A DOUBLE THIRST

Louise

With all my love,

Tess

15th August 2001

A DOUBLE THIRST

REACHING BEYOND SUFFERING

IVAN MANN

I saw in Christ a double thirst.

Mother Julian of Norwich,
Revelations of Divine Love

DARTON · LONGMAN + TODD

FOR JACKIE AND ELAINE

First published in 2001 by
Darton, Longman and Todd Ltd
1 Spencer Court
140–142 Wandsworth High Street
London SW18 4JJ

ISBN 0-232-52382-7

A catalogue record for this book is available from the British Library.

Designed by Sandie Boccacci
Phototypeset in $9^1/_2$/$12^1/_4$pt Palatino by Intype London Ltd
Printed and bound in Great Britain by
Page Bros, Norwich, Norfolk.

CONTENTS

ACKNOWLEDGEMENTS

No book is written in isolation. There are people who have a direct influence but also those who in our memories and life story have always played a significant part. They have shaped our lives, our way of thinking. I acknowledge them all.

Of the people I would particularly like to acknowledge three need special mention. Eilish Heath has been a constant friend and inspiration. Caroline Hallett's friendship too has been an enormous support. They both have read and commented on the script and made valuable comments. Revd Paul Holland is not only a good friend and inspiration but also had the insight, having read Chapter 2, to suggest a title. I am grateful to them all.

My own children too have been an inspiration as they have lived their lives. They are held in love, as always.

The editors at DLT – Florence Hamilton, Helen Porter and Katie Worrall – have done good work making clear some of my more opaque passages. I am appreciative of their skill. I am thankful too to Sheila Cassidy for her generosity.

Last but not least I am grateful for all that I have gained from books and to those who have kindly given me permission to reproduce their works here. They are acknowledged in detail in the endnotes.

INTRODUCTION

Several years ago I was facing a very difficult time in my life and as I prepared to lead worship one Sunday came across a few words that made me stop in my tracks. 'Let us pray that the Church in every land may teach men (*sic*) how to use suffering'.[1] The words have stayed with me and this book is the outcome. It is quite simply a book of reflection on how suffering might be used in the life of faith. Somehow we need to explore this question if we are to engage with the whole of life; not just for ourselves but for the sake of the world. It's my belief that the more we come to terms with our own suffering the more solidarity we show with the suffering of the world, and the more compassion we have for others.

None of this is intended to glorify suffering or to suggest that people need to suffer in order to grow. It is simply an attempt to be real about the suffering we know in ourselves, which we see in those around us, and in the world. It is an attempt to locate that suffering within the Christian understanding of God.

'My subject is War, and the pity of War' writes Wilfrid Owen[2], 'The poetry is in the pity'. My subject is suffering, and the pity of suffering. My subject is God, a God whose compassion enters suffering by suffering himself, a God who gives and receives love. My subject too is the human response to suffering.

> Taste of pity as people stare,
> Love, lots of love from mother,
> Pills you find as lasting prayer,
> An irate person may possibly
> Have faith, instead of despair.[3]

'An irate person may possibly have faith'. Any book which explores the dark mystery of suffering should perhaps begin with anger and not with smooth words. In the face of all the genocide, atrocities and disasters in the whole bloody history of mankind, perhaps anger is a better ally. Anger, transformed, gives us energy for action and not just food for thoughtful reflection. Many books about suffering have not touched the depths of anger and despair that I have experienced in the relatively minor traumatic events I have gone through. It is too easy to seek to pour oil on troubled water – and religious oil at that – rather than calm the causes of the storm.

When I began to write this book I wanted to distance myself from suffering that I might connect with it at a deeper level. That is still my intention but as I continued I realised that in trying to keep a safe distance I lost the essential anger that transformed my concern into real and gritty struggle with the whole issue of suffering. I fell into safe religious clichés and reading the earliest draft I cringe at some of my writing. In the course of its revision, the book has become a much more personal reflection on the nature of suffering. Much of it stems from a five–year period in my life which ended with the death of my first wife, Jackie. It also stems from my being available to people as someone who listens. That experience is conveyed in 'cameos' and interspersed throughout the text. I have learnt a lot from book-companions and Brian Keenan's *An Evil Cradling* stands out as a constant friend. I have let these companions speak for themselves.

It would be presumptuous to write a theoretical book about the suffering of others. I cannot speak for the victims of holocaust, earthquake, violence and war. None of those things are within my experience, but I have known suffering in my life and I have sat alongside others who suffer. This book is written for all who reflect on the suffering that life can bring and who want to offer up that reflection to be used for others so that the texture of our lives may be the stuff of eternity.

My own life journey is in the Christian tradition and much of what I say alludes to that tradition and to its spirituality and scripture. I hope that this book is not just for those who follow a similar spiritual tradition, but for all who walk the path of suffering and who struggle with its meaning and use.

IVAN MANN
March 2000

1

SUFFERING IN OUR LIVES

About suffering they were never wrong,
The Old Masters: how well they understood
Its human position; how it takes place
While someone else is eating or opening a window or just
    walking dully along;
How, when the aged are reverently, passionately waiting
For the miraculous birth, there always must be
Children who did not specially want it to happen, skating
On a pond at the edge of the wood:
They never forgot
That even the dreadful martyrdom must run its course
Anyhow in a corner, some untidy spot
Where the dogs go on with their doggy life and the torturer's
    horse
Scratches its innocent behind on a tree.[1]

In his poem *Musée des Beaux Arts* W.H.Auden catches the pathos of
the everyday suffering that goes on within our lives, suffering that
does not necessarily gain attention but which nevertheless may 'pare
us down' so that 'there is no longer enough of myself for me.'[2]

I remember sitting in a dentist's waiting room. It must have been
something in my face which invited another patient to talk to me.
She told me how it felt to look after her husband, who was dying.
'It's as though,' she said, 'my life is being drained away in order to
keep his going'. The words stuck in my mind – life being poured
out for life. And, though she did not know it, I was in the same
situation of caring for my wife who was terminally ill. Whatever
our faith or belief system, we have to find ways of dealing with
suffering. Some will know greater personal suffering, others will be
victims of the world's tragedies and barbarities, whilst others will
suffer by knowing the agony of powerlessness as they accompany
others.

In this chapter we take a look at everyday suffering which we all experience. We try to locate it within the life of faith and look at the response of love and trust.

SUFFERING IN THE TEXTURE OF OUR LIVES

Hans Kung asks, 'Is not everyone in fact hanging on his own cross?'[3] Yes, we all hang on our own cross when life holds us where we do not wish to be, or when being where we are or where we feel called to be involves pain, rejection, misunderstanding, crippling poverty and trauma.

The suffering we are asked to bear in our lives is not what we have looked for, nor is it always dramatic. It has been said that our suffering, our cross, 'is not given to us a whole visible instrument, but in bits of matchwood and sawdust'. There's no need then to identify our suffering with a particular ailment, difficult person or situation. It is more than any of these. It's the everyday suffering that comes our way because we are who we are and, for some of us, the suffering we bear because we seek to follow Jesus. Like Jesus with the cup in Gethsemane, we cannot refuse to carry some of our suffering without losing something of ourselves. In my own life I have known such moments:

Turning point –

In Gethsemane,
Father, let this cup pass me by.

Recognition –

This cup is me
It cannot pass me by.

'This cup is me'. Sometimes suffering cannot be alleviated. It is in the fibre of our being; we feel the tension in our bodies, in the pit of our stomach, in a body damaged by accident or disease. There's no denying the pain, and bearing it may be costly in the extreme. There is no sense in glorifying suffering, in pretending that suffering necessarily makes us holy. Our hope is in the possibility of suffering being redeemed. We have a part to play in the way we respond to suffering, and in the way that – though helpless ourselves – we allow God to bring something out of it.

We're not called to carry our cross valiantly, proudly, victoriously – what God requires is not gritted teeth and fine words. What God requires is simply our consent to carry our cross, however weakly – to bear the suffering that remains when we have alleviated the suffering that we can, without denying the truth of our being or the direction of our calling.

Religion itself can prevent us giving that consent. It's too easy to slip into the language of the victory of the cross. It takes courage to accept that suffering may, for a while, be the way we are being called to follow Christ. It takes wisdom to know when such suffering is not to be avoided or fought, but is to be used. It takes gentleness to lift our cross in faith and hope when life seems to be offering only pain and loss.

In the early stages of suffering from motor neurone disease, my wife watched her body begin to weaken long before the diagnosis was given. She knew herself to be on a slide. Eventually the specialist had the courage to tell her she would have four or five more years of life. Friends tried to persuade her to seek healing. Her intuition was telling her to accept. Later she was to write:

Today
I face
death.

This disease, once creeping silently,
Now gallops callously.
I am seen to stumble
and we are all embarrassingly aware.

But today
I also have
a choice.

Life is now like being on
a children's slide at the park.
There is only one direction to go in.
I am falling,
and I can't get off.
I am sliding into eternity.

But I can let go of the sides
And lift my face
To feel the sun's caress,
the wind in my hair.

And, as I go,
scatter the fresh spring flowers
from my lap
to those who care to
stop
and watch
and
enjoy the fun.[4]

The words are courageous but there's no denying the depth of suffering. Somehow consenting to bear it gives the possibility of reaching beyond it to find a greater freedom. In such acceptance is revealed something of God's freedom, giving us insight into a deeper life even in the crucifixion of our present one.

CRUCIFIXION

The man was distraught. His child was seriously ill and could die. He wanted company – somebody to talk to. He thought about his friends, wondering who could listen well to his fears and questionings. Eventually he remembered a man in church who seemed to have a quiet understanding and a firm faith. It became usual for the two to meet every week or so. In time the crisis passed and the conversations served a deeper need. Having poured out his pain and grief, the man learnt to let go of easy answers and began to find answers that made sense of his experience. In the safety of his new found friend's understanding he began to explore his way of looking at God. No longer was God a distant power, nor was he a bosom pal. He was quite simply God, and he was forgiving and accepting and sharing the pain.

Suffering has the potential to strip us of false images of God and of ourselves, until in the end we come naked before a naked God. We come with nothing before the crucified, who himself has nothing. Gone are the painted images of a Christ decently covered in a neat loincloth, gone are the images of Christ on a cross slightly higher and larger than the others. Instead, Jesus hangs on a cross just like all the others. The heat and stench that overwhelm them overwhelms him too. He knows the excruciating thirst and longing for breath that others know. The total pain that others feel, he feels too, abandonment wringing from him cries of desolation. The suffering of others is his suffering and his suffering theirs, bound together as they are in dying and death. Yet all the while the horses scratch their innocent behinds and the dogs go on with their doggy lives.

The cross is, at that time and in that place, very ordinary. Yet it becomes extraordinary. Freedom is reigning from the tree – a freedom that suffers the pain and anguish, that rails against God and yet forgives, that suffers separation from loved ones and yet gives them each other. There is in this suffering a gracious tenderness which is not in contrast to the suffering but is borne of it. I have sat alongside many who have died. It is always ordinary and yet extraordinary. There are some who, by a gift of grace both human and divine, make of the narrowing limitations of life a spacious place for others and who discover a way of 'letting go' that transcends their former selves.

The possibility of transforming our suffering lies in allowing God to enter the reality of our lives as we come to terms with what has happened to us, what is happening to us. We shall return to this theme at the end of this first chapter. There is in this an assumption that suffering is part of the texture of our lives – that somehow all our suffering can be used by God to draw us to him, that crucifixion and resurrection are intertwined. This book does not attempt to explain why suffering happens. The question seldom has a satisfactory answer, especially when you are suffering greatly. Instead it attempts to locate suffering in the life of faith. From this place of living with suffering in others and in ourselves perhaps the most crucial theology emerges.[5]

Suffering is a fact of life. It is the response of love and trust that interests me – the ability to accept and use that which cannot be alleviated, the suffering which is intrinsic to our being ourselves, or which is caused by our being true to the path we believe life has for us.

THE RESPONSE OF LOVE AND TRUST

She knew all about the man in the hospital bed suffering from cancer. She had listened to him when he was well and when he was depressed. She knew the depths to which he could go. Now, he slept.

How could she speak to him of God's love, and how could she suggest trust?

Quite simply, she couldn't. Not yet – in God's good time maybe. All she could do was renew her own love and trust and be there ready to listen and accept, to watch and wait. That was the whole of her prayer.

The image reveals a truth – suffering so often isolates. Someone who can reach out beyond themselves despite their own helplessness and powerlessness in the face of suffering can make all the difference. This reaching out beyond ourselves, this self-giving love, is the other side of bearing the cross – bearing Christ's love for others.

The priest could not imagine what to say at the funeral. The girl was only eleven. Disabled all her life, she had never spoken a word. He looked around the crowded church – so many people who had been touched by this young life. It was then that he understood. He began the address, 'Jane's life is a mystery. Of her it can be said that she was amazingly gifted for she evoked a depth of love that some of us would not have known possible . . .' Heads nodded. People understood.

To celebrate love in the face of suffering is to free oneself from the prison of suffering. It denies suffering the ability to define the whole of our life, but it does not belittle or hide the power of suffering. A moving example is that of Brian Keenan and John McCarthy. Their bantering camaraderie saw them through some difficult times in their ordeal. Their practical love for each other reached beyond their suffering. Brian Keenan writes of how his suffering evoked John's tenderness:

> I often thought how having to live beside a man so ill and watch his illness and his helplessness is almost as bad for those who watch as for those who suffer. . . . John's unremitting ministrations revealed another side of him to me. The buffoon, the fool, the comic, was a man of vast tenderness, a man of compassion. His buffoonery hid this tender part of himself that he would not normally display. . . . I wondered frequently how much of oneself does one give away or can one give away even to a suffering companion. During one of those long afternoons I lay, pain twisting and turning in my gut . . . Through the mangle I went, and was stretched and pulled. I believed John thought I was sleeping, then I felt his hand lie gently on my stomach, and it remained there. He was praying. I was overcome. I was lost for words again. I wanted to join him in prayer, I wanted to thank him for this huge and tender gesture. It revealed more courage than my battling with the guards.[6]

Seven years later Brian wrote of this incident again:

> I thought of our time together in Beirut when I had been

seriously ill and John had been anxious that I might die within a few days. His ministrations to me then had been unrelenting and deeply moving. On one occasion, I remember him placing his hands on my stomach and praying earnestly for my recovery. I smiled to myself... I would never forget that moment.[7]

Here is an image of immense love and trust which reveals itself as a transforming encounter with giftedness in another person. Clearly it was for Brian Keenan a moment of love 'with skin on', a time that sustained him. It needs no religious words to explain it. It needs only understanding as we live alongside others.

Love and trust on this scale requires no Herculean efforts to believe. It requires only courage to *reach beyond ourselves* and discover that which is within each one of us.

Suffering on a wider scale – earthquakes, racial violence, murder and genocide cannot be smoothed down by fine words, however eloquent. This random and devastating suffering is enough to make many people reject belief in God. It's understandable. Sometimes disbelief and anger is the only honest response. At such times we need people who say little but love much, who reaffirm our humanity in the face of inhumanity. In 1989 at the memorial service after the Lockerbie disaster the moderator of the general assembly of the Church of Scotland preached a memorable sermon:

> But there has been not only suffering here, there has been courage and sacrifice and understanding and compassion. A whole community reaching out with open hearts and open homes and willing hands to sustain and comfort those who have suffered loss.... Where was God in all of that? Can anyone doubt that he was right there in the midst of it? If here in the midst of evil we find goodness, if here in the midst of darkness we find light, if here in the midst of desolation, we find ourselves strangely comforted, can we doubt that our lives are touched by the God of all comfort?.... we are not helped by smooth words spoken at a safe distance, but by those who have known the darkness and are prepared to share it with us, and hold us till we see the light. That is the way the comfort of God touches and holds us.[8]

We find God in the way that people respond to suffering. That's often the way and the question becomes not why we suffer but how we respond and what meaning we give to suffering.

Love and trust begin to give meaning to suffering, begin to enable us to respond and even to use suffering. Love and trust enable us to exercise a freedom even in suffering so that we treat others and ourselves not as victims but as people who are able to give as well as receive.

Even when we are suffering we want to do as well as be done to. We want to make choices even if at times the choices are not about what is happening, but about the meaning we attach to what is happening and to the response we make. So we reach beyond ourselves and beyond suffering.

In this we see clues as to God's response to suffering in his world. God grieves for his broken world. He longs for its healing and reconciliation. He works through love and in love affirms our humanity. In Christ he enters the limitations that we know. God reaches out beyond himself in love. God risks himself, revealing the vulnerability of real love. He does not cling to his own security, does not protect himself from what his world can do, but looks for its response. In his incarnation, in entering the wood of the crib and of the carpenter's home, he foreshadows the wood of the cross.

In that crucifixion, on that wood, God is supremely reaching beyond himself in order to share the suffering of his world, not just in the suffering at Calvary but in the suffering of his people *at every time* and *in every place*. We shall look more in chapter 3 at this 'completion' of the sufferings of Christ.

'THAT THE CHURCH IN EVERY LAND MAY TEACH MEN (*SIC*) HOW TO USE SUFFERING'[9]

To hold together a belief in the love of God and an openness to the suffering of the world is to become a meeting place where healing can happen. It is to stand at the place of the cross. It is a place of prayer and of action, a place where we continually need to root our own love and trust in God, but also to be available to others. It can feel like a place of contradiction, of tension and of challenge. In the bewilderment brought about by sudden and intense suffering it is not unusual for it to be experienced as a place of numbness, loss and anger.

To be at this place where love and pain meet is to know the risk and vulnerability of love. It is a place of forces that feel like inward nails converging – a place to which we may be called by God or into which we are thrust by the circumstances of life. Sometimes the forces are so strong that we give way to despair and only later find the inner resources that enable us to begin to respond from love and trust. Sometimes we are able to remove ourselves from such a potentially destructive situation.

When we are at this place where we feel called to be or about which we have no choice – a place where love and pain coexist – we may discover paradoxically that God is to be found in both, at least that has been my experience:

> Love, for me, is entering the
> pain at the heart of my being
> and pain is entering the love
> at the centre of my being . . .
> and in both I meet my Lord . . .
> and from both I shy away –
> afraid of being overcome,
> overwhelmed.
> But as I gaze at the cross
> love, He, Jesus,
> leaves me no choice.
> Again and again I walk into the love,
>   into the pain,
> and there find myself at home again.

These words are written with hesitation for they are so easily misunderstood, but they contain a truth of the spiritual life about the way of suffering.[10]

It is true that when love and pain coexist, compassion for others is the overflow. Those who have experienced great tragedy and have not been driven to retaliation or bitterness will develop a greater understanding and constructive sympathy for others. They will hold out the possibility of love and acceptance to those who in their pain expect only rejection and further humiliation. They will be aware of their own vulnerability and their limits in being there for other people. Somehow in themselves they will hold together 'two abiding facts: unreconciled pain and unexhausted compassion.'[11] They will do this not in their own strength for the cost is too high. They will do this by identifying with Love crucified.[12]

And all this is rooted so often in the ordinariness of daily living, even if the original suffering was most extraordinary and brutal.

The two were visiting the Sandham Memorial Chapel at Burghclere where

Stanley Spencer had painted scenes from the first world war. As they drove home the one said to the other, 'Isn't it strange that a memorial to that most bloody of wars should be so domestic in its portrayal'. It was a comment that led the other to ponder long and hard about how we redeem suffering not by avoiding it but by allowing it to be expressed and to be transformed in its expression.

Spending time looking at Spencer's pictures highlights many of the themes of this chapter – the way that suffering can be eased by maintaining a humane approach to oneself and others, the way that reaching beyond oneself in love for others may transform suffering and the recognition that maybe creative portrayal of suffering may help it find a place in our lives whereby it enhances us without denying suffering's destructive power.

Of painting the Chapel Spencer wrote, 'The Burghclere memorial redeemed my experience from what it was; namely something alien to me. By this means I recover my lost self.'[13]

The paintings take us through Spencer's war beginning with his time at the Beaufort Hospital. There, as a ward orderly, he found creativity and individuality crushed, 'the usual visitors to the hospital passed us orderlies by as though we were a row of bedpans'[14]. He found too the horror of watching another's madness, and his own search for meaning. He would soon sign up for Royal Army Medical Corps service overseas.

His first posting was to Macedonia. Macedonia was to have a profound effect upon him. 'I was entranced by the landscape . . . It was not a landscape, it was a spiritual world.'[15] It was a landscape which influenced his painting greatly. Personally the sheer speed of change challenged him. 'Change; but more outrage than change . . . One is going beyond as a human what one is made by God to do. One should grow with experience, and one does not that at that artificial speed'.[16] He found himself fascinated by detail – 'the white shells of tortoises burned in grass fires, or Bulgarian letters, photographs and picture postcards scattered about the ravines.'[17] In his painting it was important to Spencer to redeem all of this suffering. Perhaps that's why in the central image of the resurrection there are two tortoises to be seen. In the inhumanity of war and suffering these 'domestic details' keep a link with the universal in man. In the wall frieze which illustrates this time there are many such de-tails – the washing of a shirt, of mess tins, of Spencer himself collecting rubbish. These touches of humanity deny suffering and darkness the power to completely define a situation.

The wall frieze on the other side of the chapel reflects a time of inactivity, of communion with nature, of waiting. But soon Spencer transferred to the infantry. He was still searching for meaning, 'being with the soldiers in that place yet had some integral meaning with other meaningful things I felt in myself.'[18] He had experienced shelling and bombing, had been up to the front line to retrieve the wounded and he had buried the dead. As an infantryman he was to know too the tension of the call to attack. On September 17 1918 a British attack had led to losses in the British sector of 165 officers and 3000 other ranks. Against that background the 7th Royal Berks were given the order forward. At the end of a nine hour march along the Sedemli ravine near Smol, Spencer was astonished to find their mail had followed them.' When in the midst of some inhuman happenings there is suddenly this need to supply all the supposedly human needs . . . it is a bit ominous . . .'[19] In fact the Bulgars retreated and the attack never happened.

SUFFERING, MEANING AND REDEMPTION

In all of this we see Spencer's yearning to find meaning in what he experiences and observes and he points us to the reality that much of our suffering can only be endured. Give the opportunity it can be redeemed at a later date by reflecting on it and learning from it. Many of his paintings at Burghclere illustrate this understanding. In *Scrubbing the floor*, an orderly rushes down a corridor whilst a patient slowly and methodically scrubs the floor. Spencer is drawing us to the need to contemplate, to take things in. Whilst the orderly has no time, the person washing the floor has a 'brief chance to "catch hold of a little bit of spiritual life"'.[20] In *Washing lockers* Spencer is kneeling, hidden between two baths, again taking opportunity to reflect.

Spencer's own reflection leads him to a monumental painting of resurrection, a painting that dominates the chapel that sees Christ not as Judge but as all compassion, all merciful. The soldiers carry their white and startling crosses to Christ. There is immense identification with Christ. On a wagon a young soldier is seen gazing at his cross which alone is a crucifix, bearing the image of Christ. Lower down almost life-sized figures emerge from their graves and reach out to each other.

Here is a picture which captures the essence of this chapter. Suffering is part of the texture of life, and some suffering is overwhelming and all we can do is endure. Suffering can be redeemed by a response of love and trust – a reaching out beyond ourselves. Identification with Christ is not a cop-out but one of the ways we exercise our freedom in assigning meaning to our suffering and making choices even in life's darkest places.

2

ALLEVIATING SUFFERING

Sorrow and Joy:
striking suddenly on our startled senses
seem, at the first approach, all but impossible
of just distinction one from the other:
even as frost and heat at the first keen contact
burn us alike.

Joy and Sorrow,
hurled from the height of heaven in meteor fashion,
flash in an arc of shining menace o'er us.
Those they touch are left
stricken amid the fragments
of their colourless, usual lives.

Imperturbable, mighty,
ruinous and compelling,
Sorrow and Joy
– summoned or all unsought for –
processionally enter.
Those they encounter
they transfigure, investing them
with strange gravity
and a spirit of worship.

Joy is rich in fears:
Sorrow has its sweetness.
Indistinguishable from each other
they approach us from eternity,
equally potent in their power and terror.

From every quarter
mortals come hurrying:
part envious, part awe-struck,
swarming, and peering
into the portent;

where the mystery sent from above us
is transmuting into the inevitable
order of earthly human drama.

What then is Joy? What then is Sorrow?
Time alone can decide between,
when the immediate poignant happening
lengthens out to continuous wearisome suffering;
when the laboured creeping moments of daylight
slowly uncover the fullness of our disaster
Sorrow's unmistakable features.

Then do most of our kind
sated, if only by the monotony
of unrelieved unhappiness, turn away from the drama,
disillusioned, uncompassionate.

O ye mothers, and loved ones – then, ah, then comes your
hour, the hour for true devotion.
Then your hour comes, ye friends and brothers! Loyal hearts
can change the face of Sorrow, softly encircle it with love's most
gentle unearthly radiance.'[1]

In these verses Bonhoeffer captures the passion, the power, and the
devastation that both joy and sorrow can bring. He conveys the need
for compassion and companionship so that all may be encircled
with 'love's most gentle unearthly radiance.'

In this chapter we explore the relationship between joy and
sorrow. We focus on personal suffering though some of the insights
gained may be applied, in different ways, to wider arenas of suffering. We ponder the nature of suffering and consider some possible
responses to it – not only in terms of the 'active' response, but also
the 'passive' response of the inner person who may discover ways
of living with suffering in such a way as to grow beyond it. This is
not to imply a kind of pious or moral sanctity wrought by passing
through the fires of suffering. It may well be far less heroic –
someone may be devastated, angry, sullen, withdrawn and miser-
able but nevertheless maintain a reality in the face of their suffering
which speaks of true holiness. This attitude is open and ready to
attend to the reality of those feelings whilst being prepared to move
on rather than to be held hostage to them.

JOY AND SORROW

If we could separate that which gives us pleasure from that which gives us pain; if we could restrict life's ability to stretch us and make us grow; if we could say that *only* joy makes us creative then we could wage all-out war on suffering and declare it useless. Much suffering is totally destructive and should be alleviated at all costs, but some suffering can be the means by which we are transformed. Sometimes that just happens and sometimes it cannot happen until we consciously consent to learn from our suffering.

There are times when what at first seems total joy gives way to intense suffering. At other times what begins as a devastating blow gives way to a maturity of living and loving which deepens rather than denies the reality of love. Again, I am reflecting on the experience of looking after my wife who had motor neurone disease. The diagnosis was given and the prognosis was poor. We drove home in silence, each wishing to protect the other from the sheer cliffs of fear and apprehension that could so easily have engulfed us. 'No worst there is none. Pitched past pitch of grief.'[2] Our life together had a time limit; not thirty or forty years, but three or four. How much God was asking!

By the time that she died Jackie had grown out of recognition. She had established her own identity in a way she had not managed to do before. I had found resources within myself and in God I barely thought possible. It had been hell but it had been heaven too and I could be at peace in entrusting her to God.

We cannot separate joy and sorrow, peace and suffering. It is for this reason that we sometimes have to live with the interplay of the many and complex encounters between our inner and outer worlds. Our response to such a multifaceted conversation may be simple but not, if it is to be real, simplistic. It may not be possible to find the 'answer' but we may need to look for answers – partial incomplete answers which together make for life and growth.

THE NATURE OF SUFFERING

The man was elderly but still very active. He thought nothing of gardening all day, of driving his car into town, of keeping in touch with world affairs and local issues. But then he had a car accident. He broke an arm and shook himself up. Fortunately nobody else was involved.

The immediate cause of his suffering was obvious, but there were

others – his failing eyesight, his loss of concentration, his increasing
inability to remember changes to the road layout and to adjust to a new
car with controls slightly different from the one he had before.

He had, as a result of the accident, a number of pains. There was not
only the physical pain of his broken arm and bruised torso but also the
pain of loss of self esteem, and the pain of the fear of isolation now that he
could no longer drive.

This simple example highlights the way that suffering has mani-
fold causes, some more deep-seated and intractable than others. In
recognising many areas and causes of suffering in a person's life –
what we shall later define as 'multifaceted suffering' – we make it
possible to address *some* of them and therefore give hope, even
though we cannot necessarily address *all* of them.

Again, let me give a personal example. When Jackie was ill, it
was easy for her illness to become the main focus of attention. In
fact her illness had many facets – physical deterioration, multiple
losses of role and aspirations, the practical losses of my job, tied
housing, income and far more. But there would be other areas of
pain too – infections, other illnesses, bereavements – that would be
invasive particularly to her. In addition, there were other life events
which had a cumulative effect on us all – two very close friends
died in their forties, another family member was diagnosed with a
neurological condition, an aunt developed breast cancer and then
leukaemia.

There were times when I was reminded of a tree I had seen at
Addington Palace. Many of the branches had been propped up with
the dead trunks of other trees. If our life were that tree then many
of the props were being removed one by one. The loss of those
props was not the direct result of Jackie's illness but they certainly
had a massive effect on our total situation. At times it felt that only
the main trunk remained, and we wondered sometimes whether we
could keep the roots steady and the tree balanced.

In such a situation hopelessness could so easily have prevailed.
Instead we had to find ways of redefining our hopes, making our
hopes smaller in scale and achievable. This included ensuring that
Jackie could maintain her interest in clothes and art, and that she
could take part in planning family celebrations. Maybe, as Martin
Israel says:

> There is some desolation that is not relieved ... easily ... It
> goes on, and any point of hope assumes the nature of a frank

illusion. No one who deals with patients suffering from motor neurone disease or inoperable cancer can escape this experience . . .[3]

Though with some conditions hope of a recovery may be in vain other hopes can be fostered in order to allay hopelessness and in order to maintain quality of life for all involved. The reaction of professionals can unwittingly set the pattern, as I discovered when I met two people who were diagnosed with motor neurone disease at about the same time as each other. The GP of one said that there was nothing he could do but to call on him if he was needed. The GP of the other called regularly to establish whether any symptoms could be alleviated or any unnecessary worries eased. One was the response of absence and the other of presence, one encouraged hopelessness and the other hope.

It is a stark reminder that a creative response to suffering is aided when we look not just for the alleviation of the prime cause but when we can respond constructively to other causes and symptoms. Alleviation is not just about cure. It is about respecting humanity even when there is no cure.

'CREEPING INHUMANITY'

Failure to recognise multifaceted suffering or to respond to it can lead to a creeping inhumanity. By 'creeping inhumanity' I mean that level of inhumanity which one person or group shows to another, not by conscious choice but by passive acquiescence to a situation in which inhumanity becomes inevitable. At a personal level this may be exemplified by our response to the elderly who suffer from dementia. Gradually the things that make a person a person are eroded – the ability to make choices, self-respect, decision-making, comprehension and memory. To live with people like that can be immensely demanding and gradually it may happen that both the person concerned and those surrounding them lose respect for humanity. This process is seldom a conscious choice but creeps in as exhaustion and frustration mount. It is damaging to all concerned. It happens over a period and becomes 'normal'. Its very insidiousness is its power and so easily risks maltreatment.

In a masterly account of the morality of the twentieth century, Jonathan Glover[4] describes how the moral identity of peoples and nations is often caught up in a gradual change, the effect of which is only realised with hindsight. 'People slide by degrees into doing things they would not do if given a clear choice at the beginning'.[5] For example, 'There was no single moment when the policy of developing the atomic bomb for use against Japan was adopted. As with the British bombing of German civilians, moral doubts were weakened by the decisions being phased.'[6]

Individually and corporately the failure to take responsibility for our moral identity[7] and to become aware of all that shapes, forms and distorts that identity means that we can unknowingly contribute to the suffering of the world. Conversely, paying attention to our moral identity, allowing it to be formed by what we would choose to be central in our lives may enable us to be more aware of the effects of our actions and more ready to speak out against common assumptions and prejudices. Alongside our moral identity our human responses[8] need to be practised in ways that respect our own limits and have compassion for our own frailty as well as in reaching out to others.

Being aware of creeping inhumanity, and revealing it for what it is, forms part of a wider response to suffering by which hope may be engendered. It emphasises the need to maintain and value our moral identity and our human responses. In the face of the manipulation of the public view by those with vested interests it's important that we maintain our own responsibility for these things.

We need to question where our deepest allegiance lies. What it is that lies at the heart of our conscience – the good of ourselves, our family, our town or nation, our religion, our status or whether we dare to go beyond partial groupings in order to make a deeper connection? As Jonathan Glover says:

> Many 'moralities' are internal, giving weight to those inside a community, but doing little against the common indifference or even hostility towards those outside. It is increasingly obvious that this moral gap is a human disaster.[9]

MULTIFACETED SUFFERING

People who seek to help those who suffer soon discover that there are many causes of suffering, and that the person who is suffering contributes greatly to their own well-being by their own attitudes and abilities. The alleviation of suffering is not just about the rich helping the poor, or the knowledgeable the ignorant, or the well-fed the hungry. It is much more to do with people being there with, for, and alongside the other as they recognise a common humanity.

Various authors have recognised the many dimensions or facets of suffering. Dame Cicely Saunders, honoured as the founder of the modern hospice movement, defined a concept of 'total pain' which she described as having 'physical, emotional, social and spiritual components' and she suggested that unless each of these was tackled, pain relief was unlikely.[10]

Simone Weil, too, sees many aspects of what she terms 'affliction'. She writes: 'There is not real affliction unless the event which has seized and uprooted a life attacks it directly or indirectly, in all its parts, *social, psychological* and *physical*.'[11] (my italics).

In recognising the many facets of suffering along with the awareness of the role of the person who is suffering we can define 'multifaceted suffering':

> To recognise multifaceted suffering is to attend to a whole person in the many dimensions of their life and the many facets of suffering within that life. It is also to acknowledge and nurture all that contributes to the well-being of that person, both from within them and without.

Clearly in a crisis or acute situation, the immediate cause of suffering needs to be alleviated but in much of life the broader approach may lead to a greater and more lasting alleviation.

RESPONSE TO MULTIFACETED SUFFERING

In responding to multifaceted suffering it is clear that a number of responses are necessary. It has been said, for instance, that 'the complex demands of palliative care cannot be adequately met through the isolated strivings of individual health care workers.'[12] There is then a need for those with appropriate skills and opportunities to play a part in a larger picture of care. This image is a helpful one in the alleviation of suffering on a wider scale. The task is not for an individual to alleviate suffering but to *play a part* in the alleviation of suffering. In doing this we contribute to the well-being of others and the well-being of society as a whole without, ourselves, being overwhelmed by the demand.

What becomes clear is that the alleviation of suffering becomes a *shared* responsibility involving a formal and informal network of professionals and non-professionals. It may embrace both traditional and complementary therapies, statutory, charitable and familial sources of help[13] . . . a broad spectrum of response to a broad spectrum of need.

Within our definition of multifaceted suffering it becomes clear that a key role is to be played by the person who is suffering. As far as possible they should 'call the shots'.

> More and more studies have shown that positive feelings – such as hope and optimism and a sense of control over one's life – can have a powerful effect on a patient's health and quality of life.[14]

For this to be possible the person needs to be well-informed about the nature of their suffering – a subject we explore more deeply when we consider 'meanings' towards the end of this chapter.

THE 'PASSIVE' RESPONSE TO SUFFERING

Beyond the practical alleviation of suffering – what we have earlier called the active response – there is also the passive response. For 'passive' do not read 'victim'. The passive response is not just about suffering what comes our way and accepting it as fate. The passive response dares to feel the reality of what is happening to us, reflects on its meaning and implications, and then consents either to bear it, work through it or seek to avoid it. In other words the passive response is that which we make inwardly as we allow ourselves to feel the full impact of what is happening to ourselves or to others. Reflection on that impact will shape and determine our active response.

The passive response to suffering may at times comprise denial, apathy, helplessness, hopelessness, powerlessness and meaninglessness. There may be feelings of anger, aggression, fear, bewilderment, isolation, grief, shock, numbness and more.

All of these have their place and need not be negative in their outcome though the experience of them may be dire. Each may be necessary and appropriate as we seek to come to terms with and live (or die) through all that faces us. Each may have a positive or negative impact, or indeed a varying impact at different times and in different situations. There will be time to experience fully a response and *time to move on* in a dynamic of growth. Brian Keenan says of denial:

> Denial is often a necessary phase in the process of adjustment,

a normal and necessary human reaction to a crisis which is too immediately overwhelming to face head on. Denial gives time for a temporary retreat from reality, time for our internal forces to regroup and to regain strength, to begin to deal with the loss that has been forced upon us.[15]

Elisabeth Kubler-Ross, in her classic study *On Death and Dying* argues that denial is a 'healthy way of dealing with the uncomfortable and painful situation'[16] with which terminally-ill patients may live for some time. Normally, of course, denial gives way to at least partial acceptance.

Suffering in silence, the avoidance of risk, the consent (conscious or unconscious) to the loss or lessening of our own moral identity, the will to protect others – all these can be ways of denying and avoiding suffering as though ultimately we could defeat it by such means. It simply does not work and can cause more suffering, not less.

It was clear to her that the marriage was failing yet a desire to keep it going, to be faithful to the vows meant that she tried for too long to protect her husband and the children from the effects of separation and maybe of divorce. Her husband, aware of her suffering though not the extent of it, encouraged her to keep going.

Eventually she became very depressed. Torn between the demands of the family and the teaching of the church on one side, and her own awareness of the destructive effect it was having on her, she determined even more to keep going – to take the pain on herself. She failed. The whole family was being changed by her pain. Her failure only added to her depression. At the point of desperation she sought professional help. Once she had given voice to her pain and its force in her life she began to see that in this situation pain could not be avoided. It was not a case of pain or no pain. It was a matter of accepting the pain which might lead to the most constructive and sustainable outcome

Apathy, too, may be a way of dealing with too much suffering. A man who cared for his wife though years of chronic pain and paralysis brought about by ME writes:

It's strange – when someone you love is always ill, always in pain. It is impossible to sustain the hurt at a high level. You become used to witnessing pain and suffering – it's the norm, and the sadness is pitched to such a point over a long period that it is not possible to accommodate the peaks. The result is a continuing numbness that is set to a certain frequency, and the occasional crisis just bounces off.[17]

Such apathy may be necessary at times as a way of protecting ourselves from too much reality. Sometimes, though, pain breaks through and needs to break through if apathy is not to be completely paralysing.

Apathy may also express itself in hopelessness and helplessness – a form of powerlessness which can become manipulative, creating ill-feeling and tension between all involved. Powerlessness can be experienced over a long period but can be constructive. Soelle writes:

> Every attempt to humanise suffering must begin with this phenomenon of experiencing powerlessness and must activate forces that enable a person to overcome the feeling that he is without power.[18]

Eventually, if we allow ourselves to be conscious of our powerlessness, anger may emerge and be the fire that energises us to begin to exercise what power we do have, and to overturn the inhumanity that life or other people has shown us or which we have inflicted on ourselves. The alleviation of suffering is often about helping the powerless discover what power they have. It is sometimes about being the one who voices the suffering of another until they are empowered to voice it themselves – to be the 'voice of the voiceless', the one who sings suffering's lament on behalf of another.

Sometimes powerlessness is broken through by some revelation of humanity – by the ways others treat us, or by the way someone else's humanity suddenly becomes apparent. Wilfrid Owen in his poem 'Strange Meeting' speaks of a recognition of the enemy as being human, 'I am the enemy you killed, my friend.'[19] As Glover says:

> Sometimes the breakthrough is a simple emotional response, triggered by the visible reminder of someone's humanity: by the family letters and photographs of girlfriends found by soldiers in the pockets of those on the other side, or by seeing the fascist soldier holding up his trousers.[20]

Meaninglessness, though it may colour our lives slowly, yet pervasively, can destroy any sense of our own humanity having value in our life situation. This meaninglessness affects individuals at many levels – the dull routine of a job, an inevitability about sustaining an unhappy and deeply destructive relationship, the loss of self-esteem, the loss of identity that some experience as a result of grief, the sheer disbelief in anything in the face of catastrophic suffering.

In all these things what may seem to be the final straw is often the beginning of healing. It may bring the inner resolve to do or see things differently.:

MIND THE GAP

Often life reflects that impersonal voice which echoes in the railway station as the doors open to reveal a chasm between the train and the platform – mind the gap. Chasms in our lives can be frightening, especially that chasm between the way we imagine life to be, or imagine it should be, and the way life actually is. There may be a devastating chasm between the way we would aspire to live and the life that is possible. Sometimes the gap can seem too wide, the chasm too deep. Despair may seem to be a reasonable option.

Awareness of the gap, however, may mean that we take seriously the need to make choices about our life – if not about what to do then about the meanings and weight that we give to our situation. Suffering so often seems to eliminate choice from our life – we cannot change the situation so we assume that we must be content with all that is happening and that we are powerless to effect any change.

It's an assumption which needs challenging in many ways. Victor Frankl, reflecting on the experience of the concentration camps, writes:

> Man is not destroyed by suffering, he is destroyed by suffering without meaning. We need meaning to give value and order to our way of living and being. Sometimes, the meaning we give to our experience is the only choice left – but it is a choice and in the light of our faith we can review our experience, and, by allowing deeper meanings to emerge, often change the power of the past over us.[21]

Allowing meanings to emerge is perhaps the key to this – letting *different levels of meaning* emerge

At a practical level, part of the meaning we need to explore is about what is happening to us. Being well-informed about the causes of our suffering is the first step to alleviating what we can.

Conversely a long period of not knowing what is happening to us can be deeply destructive. We need to use some discernment in what we accept to be true about our condition and find trusted sources of information rather than any information we can find.

Another level of meaning is that which we give to our suffering in the light of the beliefs we hold – what we may call 'spiritual' beliefs – about life which shape our response. For some such spiritual beliefs will include formal religious beliefs; for others, not.

We do well to avoid superficial explanations, religious or otherwise. Often the meaning is not clear until we can create some distance from our suffering. Brian Keenan reminds us of the need sometimes to withdraw from others, to create our own space in order to be more aware of our own unique self. In a remarkable passage he writes of his and John McCarthy's need to find meaning:

> More and more we sought now to live our lives exclusively to ourselves and as far as possible dismiss the existence of these men and *create our own separate meaning*.[22]

Here the need to assert our distinctiveness is highlighted as a means of alleviating suffering. By so doing we give worth to our unique identity, we affirm our humanity and maintain our integrity in the face of all that assails us. As Sheila Cassidy writes of her work in a hospice:

> I am affirming the worth of an individual person in a world in which the individual is at risk of being submerged or valued only for his strength, intellect, or beauty. It is a prophetic statement about the unique value of the human person, irrespective of age, social class or productivity.[23]

As so often in life, the task is to discover what is appropriate in any situation. Keenan recognises that in the midst of chaos it is important not to allow one's identity to be defined by the chaos and to find one's own meaning if one is to survive. For him it was a conscious choice. Cassidy makes the same choice and seeks to give that same breadth of response to a patient, not defining them by their symptoms or prognosis.

Here we touch on the crux of the matter – that the meaning we give a situation is closely tied up with the value we place on individual identity. The question for those whose suffering allows for some distancing and reflection may be 'what meaning can I give this situation whereby I may best express my own unique self?' It is a question which reflects the task of alleviating suffering, the task of allowing the person who is suffering to assert their unique essence – their spirit – whatever the outward circumstances. Here freedom may be found for, as Keenan makes clear, when external circumstances restrict our freedom we can still find an inner freedom:

> Captivity had re-created freedom for us. Not a freedom outside us to be hungered after, but another kind of freedom which we found to our surprise and relish *within ourselves*.[24] (my italics).

Such freedom may be found not by stepping outside a situation but by seeing it in a different way.

> After so long, so long
> in my tight prison,
> with my familiar shackles
> heavy on head and heart;
> after so long, so long,
> suddenly I see the bars
> with the eyes God gave me,
> touch the chains
> with the hand God made me,
> and suddenly, suddenly
> (oh, but my heart flies out of the dream
> like a singing bird!),
> suddenly I am free.[25]

In order to find this healing we may need to risk letting the meaning and weight attached to a situation change in the light of experience. We may need to mind and reduce the gap. It is a risky business.

As well as letting constructive meaning emerge we may also choose, meanwhile, how much 'weight' to give to a situation. So often suffering is increased by bearing responsibility or giving weight to that which is not ours to own. We highlight a negative to the extent of blinding ourselves to the whole picture, we carry on nursing wounds from the past rather than addressing them as far as we are able and then either letting them go, or giving them less 'weight' until we can address them. There are choices to be made – choices of meaning (or indeed the choice not to give meaning), choices about whether the meaning we have given to a situation needs to be reviewed and changed and choices about the weight we give to circumstances, events and memories.

... we are constantly renewing our understandings as we change the ... meaning we place on events. ... To be faithful to this process is to risk ... a sort of bereavement when those formulations, images and symbols through which we had in the past appropriated truth have now to be abandoned. For those formulations images and symbols, over the years become part of ourselves.[26]

SMASHING OF IDOLS

Later, we shall discuss the wilderness experience as a place of smashing of idols. Sufficient to say here that part of the way we need to 'mind the gap' in order to alleviate suffering is to redefine our ideals in the light of experience. Some of the ideals that have shaped our lives may no longer be appropriate. We neither can nor should live up to them any longer. Other ideals may take their place and provide more therapeutic and enriching models for living, and a greater inner and outer freedom to be.

In redefining our ideals we can embrace other meanings to our life. As Verena Tschudin says, 'Values are closely related to meaning – the meaning of life. The inner meaning of an action, an experience or attitude gives us our values.'[27]

This redefining of ideals may be necessary not only in our present but also as we review our past.

REMEMBERING WELL

Part of the task of alleviating suffering is to live with our past so that it frees us, individually and corporately, to live the future with hope, optimism and stability – not trying to avoid the past but having integrated its lessons into our present. Remembering the past well is therefore critically important. Remembering well does not abandon the past, nor dwell in the past, but builds on it, allowing its insights and revelations to be a transforming presence in the circumstances of our lives. Such transformation may itself either prevent or alleviate suffering. We shall return later to the whole subject of remembering well.

BEARING OUR FAILURE

In this chapter we have spoken positively about the alleviation of suffering both in terms of active and practical alleviation but also in terms of the more passive and inward response that is necessary if the total picture of suffering – 'multifaceted suffering' – is to be addressed.

Such a chapter cannot end without affirming the awareness that there are some aspects of suffering that cannot be alleviated despite our best efforts and intentions. It is important to recognise this reality whilst affirming that hope may come from an appreciation of the widest possible responses, and from tapping the deepest possible inner resources.

3

SUFFERING IN OURSELVES

As Kingfishers catch fire, dragonflies draw flame;
As tumbled over rim in roundy wells
Stones ring; like each tucked string tells, each hung bell's
Bow swung finds tongue to fling out broad its name;
Each mortal thing does one thing and the same:
Deal out that being indoors each one dwells;
Selves – goes itself; *myself* it speaks and spells;
Crying *What I do is me: for that I came.*

I say more: the just man justices;
Keeps grace: that keeps all his goings graces;
Acts in God's eye what in God's eye he is –
Christ – for Christ plays in ten thousand places,
Lovely in limbs, and lovely in eyes not his
To the Father through the features of men's faces.[1]

The suffering we bear just because we are the person we are is often the least noticed. It's so much a part of the texture of our lives that we, and others, take it for granted. In extreme situations it may be that we suffer not only this everyday suffering but exceptional suffering just because of who we are and where we are. In this chapter we explore these areas of suffering and the constant need for attitudes that recognise and respect humanity in relationships and in the structures of society. We look at the suffering brought about by our 'facticity' – a word used by John Macquarrie to encapsulate all the 'givens' of any particular existence – intelligence, race, temperament, and many other factors that no-one chooses for himself. Environment and heredity, our place in history and society . . .'[2]

WHAT I DO IS ME: FOR THAT I CAME

Gerard Manley Hopkins' words are very apt. 'The cross is . . . the everyday suffering that comes our way because we are the person

that we are and because we seek to follow Jesus. Like the cup in
Gethsemane, we cannot refuse to carry it without losing something
of ourselves.'

*He was coming to terms with so much suffering in his life. It seemed
impossible to bear. A friend suggested that he go on retreat and be refreshed
in the love of God. In the silence he pondered what life was to be for him
after the loss of several people who were very significant in his life. More
than that, there was another area of his life, another cause of suffering that
no one knew anything about. He had struggled for many years with the
knowledge that he was homosexual.*

*He came across some words on the Retreat House noticeboard. They
struck him forcibly and years later, he was still pondering what they meant
for him. 'Remember, the repentance for what you do may go deep, but the
repentance for what you are goes deeper. (A. W. Tozer)'*

Hopkins' words, 'What I do is me: for that I came', are taken a
stage further – what I am is me: for that I came. When that 'me' is
unacceptable to others then I may repent of being myself. Of course
it is a vain repentance for we cannot turn away from the person
that God made us without turning away from life itself. But it can
be pretty hard to bear. Hopkins knew all about the pain of carrying
one's own nature. In September 1888 he told Robert Bridges, 'It
seems to me that I cannot always last like this: in mind or body or
both I shall give way. All I really need is a certain degree of relief
and change; but I do not think that what I need I shall get in time
to save me.'[3] Hopkins also knew the possibility of Christ living 'in
ten thousand places, lovely in limbs, and lovely in eyes not his.' He
held together both his own hopelessness and despair with the hope
of resurrection and of new life. In a retreat note made at the beginning of 1889, he writes, 'Nothing to enter but loathing of my life
and a barren submission to God's will . . .'[4] In contrast at the end of
his poem 'That Nature is a Heraclitean Fire and of the comfort of the
Resurrection' he writes of his hope of resurrection:

> In a flash, at a trumpet crash,
> I am all at once what Christ is, since he was what I am, and
> This Jack, joke, poor potsherd, patch matchwood, immortal
>   diamond,
> Is immortal diamond.[5]

This hope, which seems so at odds with his hopelessness, nevertheless found some realisation. He was ill for six weeks with typhoid before he died in June 1889. 'According to members of the College community, he was heard two or three times to say, "I am so happy. I am so happy", before he became too weak to speak.'[6] The English version of the notice of his death in the official *Register of the English Province* reads: '1889. On the eighth day of June, the vigil of Pentecost, weakened by a fever, he rested. May he rest in peace. He had a most subtle mind, which too quickly wore out the fragile strength of his body.'[7] A biographer writes:

> 'As a man he was torn apart when he was in doubt, but it was precisely when he was impelled, perhaps neurotically, to examine all aspects of a problem, including its unattractive side, that his poetry came most fully alive. Poetically, he probably thrived more on uncertainty than on unadulterated happiness, and to that extent he is a good example of that unpalatable dictum that some poets must be destroyed personally in order to be whole artistically.'[8]

Hopkins' life points to the difficult truth that suffering in ourselves can produce extreme beauty. It never seems that this excuses the suffering, but it does suggest that suffering is not entirely destructive if it can somehow be transformed into something else.[9]

FINITUDE

Hopkins points to the tension within us between having a vision of the grandeur and spaciousness of what might be possible and the limits of existence that preclude us from having that which we most desire.

> Every freedom is balance against a limitation, perhaps a limitation of power ... or perhaps a limitation of knowledge ... So existence is always characterised by the tension between possibility and facticity, between man's freedom and his manifold finitude.[10]

Indeed our freedom in a particular situation may be very slim. Our temperament, gender, race, colour, abilities, disabilities, sexual orientation in a particular situation, culture or society may mean that these elements of facticity actually restrict our freedom to nothing. One of the last freedoms to go is the freedom to make choices about the meaning and weight we attach to a situation, but in some suffering even that freedom is taken away if we experience total pain[11] or affliction. This is suffering in isolation in the extreme – something we will explore more in chapter 4. We have to remind ourselves too that some people's suffering ends in death without any choices being possible and with no opportunity to reflect on that suffering. Living with finitude is to acknowledge that we live with risk and uncertainty and with real limitations. It does not, however, excuse us from questioning whether limitations we perceive are real or self-imposed. In total pain we are beyond making choices, beyond articulation. All we can do is be, and all we can be is pain. But beyond that total pain every opportunity for choice is an opportunity for life. If we deny our ability to make choices we are colluding with that which is death-dealing and that, as has been said earlier, is a choice in itself. Not that choices offer a pain – free existence, but they do offer a sense of being 'real' in the situation, of still being a person, which is why in situations where our very humanity is under attack we especially need to be aware of choices. In the second world war a Polish priest, Maksymilian Kolbe, was in Auschwitz. One of Poland's champion boxers before the war, a man known as Teddy who was 'not given to sentimentality' speaks of Kolbe's 'crazy courage.'

> Everybody was starving and a man is an egoist when he is starving and doesn't care what is going on; all he can think about is getting a bit of bread. It was not only the last sacrifice of Maksymilian Kolbe which was remarkable but his whole behaviour in the camp. He often offered himself to be beaten in place of someone else and he always shared his rations . . . He had too great a heart . . . it was just against all reason.[12]

When humanity is offered to another in a place of inhumanity we raise ourselves above the animal kingdom and reflect the nature of God whose way is the way of courageous tenderness. Whenever one person reaches out to another in love, breaking down prejudice, discrimination, isolation and fear; whenever a person reaches out to feed the hungry, comfort the dying, attend the sick; whenever a person risks their life in order to search for others in the devastation after an earthquake or bomb we are seeing such courageous tenderness.

She was in her eighties and life had given her much pain to carry but also much love. She lay on her bed and he just listened as she told the story of

her life. She spoke of the war years and of going to bed at night knowing
that the bombers might fly over. 'There was so much love in that place
where I lived then'. There was no sentimentality here – just a recognition
that simple humanity could live even in the face of war. As she recalled so
many people who had 'been there' for her she brought blessing to herself
and he who listened.

DEATH

Being with somebody who is terminally ill can be very distressing. Simply by being there, however, even if we sometimes say and do what we later judge 'the wrong things', we have the opportunity to reveal our commitment and love.

It is a privilege to face the death of somebody who has addressed the issues that have concerned and undermined them in life. In my own case this is highlighted by an incident a few days before my wife died. We already knew that Jackie's lifespan was short – maybe days or weeks. We were in a hospital ward and found ourselves absent-mindedly watching a television programme about white-water canoeing. The presenter asked the canoeist whether he was afraid as he launched himself on the water to be carried by it through a narrow, rock-laden ravine. 'Of course I'm afraid!', he said, 'but once I start the only way out is through.'

I thought Jackie was dozing, but suddenly she came to life, and said, 'That's exactly where I am.' We were able to discuss her death together – openly and honestly and talk about the future – hers, the children's, and mine. It was a crystallisation of the previous five years during which we had faced many losses – many inner dyings – the loss of her ability to walk unaided, to walk at all, to hold her head up, to dress herself, to wash herself, the loss of our ability to go out as a family without a wheelchair, the loss of going out at all, the loss of our home and my job and income, the loss of our privacy . . . all these losses had their own grief. The final loss was not isolated. It was part of a pattern of loss, part of a process.

This is true not only of our rather intense circumstances but of life as a whole . The ability to cope with loss and change is a preparation for the loss and change of death. If we want to prepare for death the best preparation is to live fully and to get used to loss and change, always seeking the lessons and moving on from them. Indeed, the more we love life, the more we will feel keenly the losses that life brings, but also the more able we will be to grow through them. D. H. Lawrence speaks profoundly to this situation in his poem *Shadows*. He catches this sense of entering our 'dyings' with a trust in the possibility of being re-created.

And if tonight my soul may find her peace
In sleep, and sink in deep oblivion,
and in the morning wake like a new-opened flower
then I have been dipped again in God, and new created.

And if, in the changing phases of man's life
I fall in sickness and in misery
my wrists seem broken and my heart seems dead
and strength is gone, and my life
is only the leavings of a life:

and still, among it all, snatches of lovely oblivion, and snatches
of renewal,
odd, wintry flowers, upon the withered stem, yet new, strange
flowers
such as my life has not brought forth before, new blossoms of
me –

then I must know that still
I am in the hands [of] the unknown God,
he is breaking me down to his own oblivion
to send me forth on a new morning, a new man.[13]

SHARING THE HUMANITY OF ANOTHER

In chapter 2 the need to recognise our common humanity was emphasised. In considering the suffering that we bear because of our place in history this finds a keener edge, for in the devastation of countries and peoples, those who offer most hope to those who suffer are those who recognise their humanity and respond to it.

The literature of war attests profoundly to this and poets such as Wilfrid Owen and Siegfried Sassoon enable us to see this gift of shared humanity.

Wilfrid Owen writes:

Above all I am not concerned with Poetry.
My subject is war, and the pity of War.
The poetry is in the pity.[14]

In his very being he allowed the pain, horror and bloodshed to meet his own humanity and his own sense of beauty. With Sassoon's encouragement Owen produced some of the finest war poetry which has survived beyond his death.

Siegfried Sassoon was a courageous and gallant soldier with a true sense of humanity. For his men he put his life at risk gaining an MC and a stay in Craiglockhart, a neuraesthenics' hospital near Edinburgh, as a result of his Declaration in July 1917:

> I have seen and endured the suffering of the troops, and I can no longer be a party to prolonging these sufferings for ends which I believe to be evil and unjust . . . On behalf of those who are suffering now I make this protest against the deception which is being practised on them; also I believe that I may help to destroy the callous complacence with which the majority of those at home regard the continuance of agonies which they do not share, and which they have not sufficient imagination to realise.[15]

The suffering of others was ingrained in his soul and death was seeping into him. He writes:

> Soldiers are citizens of death's gray land,
> Drawing no dividend from time's tomorrows.[16]

In his diary for April 17 1917 he writes, 'Death and living were very nearly one, for death was in all our hearts.'[17] His own anguish is evident.

> I'm back again from hell
> With loathsome thoughts to sell;
> Secrets of death to tell;
> And horrors from the abyss.[18]

War makes not only soldiers 'citizens of death's gray land' but also people who have made no *choice* to fight. The loss that results from war can seldom be described in words and we become numb to images, though when we bring it down to a human level it becomes something we can identify with.

In her powerful novel *Strange Meeting* Susan Hill portrays two men and the effect of war upon them and upon their families. John Hilliard, a young subaltern, returns to the western front and 'after a brief period of sick leave back in an England blind to the horrors of the trenches, finds his battalion tragically altered.'[19] He finds himself sharing quarters with David Barton, a man only three days out of England. The novel recounts the friendship that develops between the two men and how meaningful that shared intimacy can be in the face of inhumanity.[20] It also portrays all the 'losses' of war – not only the fatalities but the relationships that are irrevocably altered. On his return to England on sick leave Hilliard is shocked by the lack of understanding and he knows himself to be changed. 'He scarcely recognised the person he had once been, the person his family seemed to remember.'[21] Immense suffering has that capacity to change us at the deepest of levels – not just in war but in everyday suffering.

In all of this there is no denial of suffering. Instead suffering is seen for what it is and finds its transformation in the lives of those who will allow it to happen. It reveals itself in a desire to bring suffering to an end, in maintaining human dignity even in suffering, and in giving a voice to suffering. Siegfried Sassoon and Wilfrid Owen encapsulated all three. In *Strange Meeting*, Susan Hill gives voice to suffering as well as to love, and in her characters she reveals the power of friendship which cannot be underestimated at such times. There is a stunning parallel between her characters and Brian Keenan and John McCarthy.

Towards the end of the novel, when David Barton has been killed and John Hilliard is going to visit David's parents, he is collected from the station by a neighbour of the Barton family, George Bennett:

> The car started, drove very slowly out of the station yard, down a slope, turned into a lane.
> 'Hob's lane,' Hilliard said. George Bennett looks surprised.
> 'That's it.'
> 'Leading to Woodman's Lane.'
> 'You've been here before then?'
> 'No.' But then he thought that that was not true, he had been here, he had spent hours here with Barton, as they had talked in the apple loft and the tents and the dugouts and billets, he could walk down the lane and paths for miles around. He knew it.
> 'No. I haven't been here before.'[22]

Brian Keenan writes:

> John's fascination with my stories of Ireland was mirrored in me as I hungrily swallowed his stories of his own home life: the beautiful Elizabethan farmhouse, its herb garden and orchard, the massive timber-beamed building which had once

been his family home ... So many times ... I could imagine myself being there. I saw myself walking past the little herb garden which might have filled the skirts of Elizabethan ladies with its aroma.[23]

Sharing in the humanity of another is vital as we go through suffering. 'We cannot know ourselves or declare ourselves human unless we share in the humanity of another.'[24] We shall explore the theme of sharing the suffering of others more in chapter 7, but now we turn to explore the suffering of our humanity.

'THE PERSON HE HAD ONCE BEEN'

In Susan Hill's novel Hilliard scarcely recognises the person he had been. This has also been my experience from being with Jackie and later going through a long and deep period of depression.

I had nursed Jackie for five years and had cared for our four small children. I had washed the baby's nappies and rejoiced when the boy learnt how not to need them. I had then had to use nappies on Jackie herself. I had worried endlessly about the family finances and found it impossible to maintain my work. Our social and sexual life had diminished. At times I was driven to the edge by sheer exhaustion and all the time tried to keep this to myself and not burden others. When Jackie died the youngest child was five and going to school. I tried to go back to living as I had before, but I had a changed understanding of myself, or had I changed deep within myself? Only years later did I accept that change and move on, stronger for it.

There's immense cost in that too, not only for the individual but for those around them. The temptation is to try to carry on being who people have come to expect you to be, but in fact it is no longer possible. You have been put through a furnace. Some of the dross has been burnt away, exposing more dross. And you have been stressed consistently over a long period.

To others you are the same person. To yourself you are partly a stranger who has yet to be befriended.[25]

WHAT WE ARE AND WHAT WE ARE BECOMING

Humour is essential if we are to enjoy the facticity – the 'what we are' of our being. There is something outrageously funny, if we dare to see it, just in being human. Alan Coren describes it well:

3. And the rib, which the Lord had taken from the man, made he a woman, and brought her *unto* the man. And the woman looked upon the man and spake, saying: typical, sleeping.

4. And the man stared at her exceeding *hard* saying; look, I have got this rib-ache, it must be the sudden digging, ye have got to take these things slowly, I have not touched a fork all winter, or it could be the weather, I have never known a March like it, it goes right through you, what are those nasty lumps on thy chest?[26]

Humour can often release us from the constraints of what we are. It can give us a new perspective and a glimpse of what we might become.

In Christian theology what we are is made clear in the story of creation.' Let us make humankind in our image, according to our likeness', says God. They are the most glorious few words for they reveal not only our being but our hope. Our being is essentially in the image of God. That image is intact. The likeness though is marred by what has traditionally been called original sin. In simple terms we may say that the likeness is marred by all that draws us away from God – not only the imperfections of our nature and nurture but also the structural sin of society. But deep down there is in us a place which God has made for himself, a place where his image can reveal itself in us as we give our consent, as we allow it to emerge.

> At the heart of my being
> is love.
> In silence I allow the
> mists to clear
> and slowly, gently
> the face of love
> – it is the face of Christ –
> comes clear
> and living water
> begins to well up
> unbidden
> in my soul
> and I am filled
> with light and love and joy . . .
> and for that time
> – maybe only the blinking of an eye,

but eternity to me –
I am home.

Now that's glorious and hopeful for if the image is there and the
marred likeness can be transformed – the basis of Christian hope[27] –
then change is no longer a threat but may actually be a part of
that transformation to be welcomed rather than feared. In secular
understandings of human nature, too, the need for change and to
see ourselves as people in process – people 'who are becoming' is
well documented.[28]

Being prepared to change and to accept change in others is fundamental to a recognition of and response to humanity – fundamental
to the ability to see difference as gift.

BECOMING WHO I AM, ACCEPTING WHO YOU ARE

To return to one of the themes of chapter 2, we can enjoy both our
connection and our distinctiveness, as well as our growth.

It is important that we allow space as well as intimacy in our
relationships in order to let change happen. That's one of the reasons
why falling in love has to give way to the grittiness of everyday
living. People in love often see in the loved one not the real person
but an image.

Falling in love with the image without allowing the real person
to emerge is bound to end in disaster and entail suffering. It is
equally true of parents and children when parents have an image
of what their child should be and cannot accept the reality.

In one way the spiritual life is nothing more than the breaking of
images, the smashing of idols, not only in the sense of letting God
be God but also in the sense of learning to love and respect other
people, however different they are. Again humour, honesty and a
trenchant spirit can combine to make the point. Sojourner Truth,
born in 1797 into slavery and a courageous campaigner for human
rights, said:

That man over there say
    a woman needs to be helped into carriages
and lifted over ditches
    and to have the best place everywhere.
Nobody ever helped me into carriages
    or over mud puddles
        or gives me a best place . . .

And ain't I a woman?
  Look at me . . .
And ain't I a woman?
  that little man in black there say
a woman can't have as much rights as a man
  cause Christ wasn't a woman.
Where did your Christ come from?
  From God and a woman!
Man had nothing to do with him!
  If the first woman God ever made
was strong enough to turn the world
  upside down, all alone
together women ought to be able to turn it
  rightside up again.[29]

Sojourner Truth is crying out for humanity to be recognised. The essential gift of humanity which God gives to each one of us has to be at the base of all relationships. 'There is no longer Jew or Greek, there is no longer slave or free, there is no longer male and female for all of you are one in Christ Jesus'.(Gal 3:28).

A CRY FOR HUMANITY

When we suffer as a result of who we are or because of the circumstances of our life – our finitude and facticity – we long for understanding and for a sense of belonging to overcome our confusion and isolation.

When this longing is intense then it's likely that conventional religious dogma, unless it has already been assimilated into a living faith, will not touch that place in us which we long to be touched. The ravine of suffering that we have travelled will not only have changed us and our self-understanding but will also have made us less accepting of easy answers.

Instead we will need to look deeper into that which is divine in all of us, to the core of humanity which links us with God and with all creation. We have to come to terms with our own weakness and powerlessness. It costs everything but should we manage to go through suffering and still be able to love then our suffering may feed into the good of others.

Keeping in touch with our humanity may see us through even the darkest times. The affliction which has affected us in all aspects – physical, psychological and societal – is eased when there are others who reveal to us compassion and maybe understanding. These people will be 'there for us' come what may and may save us from going under. The experience of suffering at this level not only reveals our weakness and powerlessness but also our darkness and shadow.

DARKNESS AND SHADOW

Some of the 'givens' of our lives are temperament and life experience. Both may be positive but our temperament will have its shadow side[30] and unresolved wounding from the past, especially if it is unacknowledged, will make itself known at times in ourselves and in our relationships. When this happens in a negative or destructive way we may call it 'darkness'. Not only do we have to live with our own shadow and darkness but also with other people's!

> In any case, community is not about perfect people. It is about people who are bonded to each other, each of whom is a mixture of good and bad, darkness and light, love and hate....there can be growth only if we recognise the potential, and this will never unfold if we prevent people from discovering and accepting themselves as they are, with their gifts and their wounds. They have the right to be rotters, to have their own dark places, and corners of envy and even hatred in their hearts. These jealousies and insecurities are part of our wounded nature. That is our reality. We have to learn to accept them and live with them.... gradually knowing ourselves to be forgiven.... There is a part of us which is already luminous... And there is a part of us which is still in shadow.[31]

We also have to live with the shadow and darkness of society, and of the created order whose warmth and wildness are untameable.

Our 'shadow' includes those aspects of our 'self' that we do not choose to value and so do not allow them space in our lives. The shadow has positive as well as negative power which we may embrace, enjoy and use, or repress. If repressed the shadow will not disappear but go underground, only to emerge when we are stressed, fatigued, or under the influence of alcohol or mind-altering drugs.[32]

Darkness – our own and that of the world – is not so easily identified. It may come upon us without warning and spin us into chaos. The struggle can be immense, as Brian Keenan testifies:

> In these conditions, there was no way to control the mind. It

spun off, launched into some unholy awfulness, doubling the physical suffering. The words and images that flash through the mind in such conditions are not of human origin, and they were beyond my understanding. They crushed me with their horror. It seemed as if hot wires were being drawn slowly through the centre of my brain. My mind was exploding over and over again.[33]

As for the darkness and shadow of the world and society, no-one helps us more than Mother Mary Clare S.L.G.:

> We have got to live now in and through the dying, in order that we may bear witness to the Resurrection life . . . If we live in this glorious perspective, we do not have to wait for the fullness of life after death. Life in God is here and now, experienced first and foremost through experiencing death. Do not be afraid to die, do not be afraid when you are overwhelmed by the sense of your own weakness and sin and muck and desolation. Let everything that is in you, and everything which is thrown up against you by the power of evil, be held in Christ's healing power. Do not absorb it or be overcome by it, but let it in you meet Christ's power to heal; let it in you meet this almighty power of God, so that in you the mess can be transformed, answered.[34]

BEFRIENDING THE SHADOW

In befriending the shadow, play is often a better solution than prayer. God delights in us and expects us to delight! Relaxation, hobbies, and sport can use parts of our personalities and temperaments that would otherwise lie dormant. By befriending them they have less hidden power over us. To return to Brian Keenan and John McCarthy, it is amazing to see how they discover the necessity of play even in captivity.[35] In contrast, Dietrich Bonhoeffer writes of how in prison games were forbidden.[36] The way is always to affirm humanity, or have it denied.

SPIRITUAL DARKNESS

Much more will be said of spiritual darkness in chapter 10. In the spiritual tradition darkness, though painful and difficult to bear, is sometimes the means by which God is trying to break in. It is not to be assumed that this is the case, however and sometimes the answer to darkness is to get out of it if you can. If you cannot then the evidence is straightforward. Stand firm, look at God, ask what God is trying to teach you. Sometimes we are reduced to sheer 'animal perseverance, or even to simply being there, like a rock, without knowing why, nor to what purpose'.[37] Using suffering is not easy. We may fail miserably to find any way of using it or bearing it; we may scream an animal scream of painful intensity.

In this chapter we have explored what it means to be human – to be mortal, and to be born into a 'givenness' which affects our whole life. We have acknowledged that out of suffering beauty, tenderness, friendship, blessing, freedom, humour may be born. The cost is not underestimated – suffering may cost us everything, even our life – nor is the darker side denied. Suffering can destroy personalities and relationships, but it is possible sometimes to not just fight suffering but to reach beyond it. One of the ways that we can reach beyond it is to give it voice, as Sassoon and Owen were able to do – a theme which forms the core of the next chapter.

4

GIVING VOICE TO SUFFERING

Thy hand, Belinda; darkness shades me.
On thy bosom let me rest.
More I would, but death invades me.
Death is now a welcome guest.

When I am laid in earth,
May my wrongs create
No trouble in thy breast;
Remember me, but ah! forget my fate.[1]

Tate's words and Purcell's music evoke a strong sense of the need
to be remembered. We want to be remembered by those we love
when we die. We like to remember those who have been special to
us – 'the memory of the righteous is a blessing'.[2] We want to be
remembered for what has been positive in our lives, for the contribution we may have made. We long not to be remembered for the
ghastly mistakes that taunt us and diminish us – the mocking voices
of our own memory. In this chapter we look at how remembering
wisely is important if we are to treasure those who have gone before
us, not just individuals but peoples, and if we are to be able to learn
all that the past can teach us as we seek to shape the present and
the future. It is not just about remembering, then, but about *how* we
remember. In the context of suffering memory is especially
important if we are to give to those who have suffered a voice – a
means of articulating what they have suffered and learnt and what
they would have us learn. We also look at how suffering can be
voiced in the present generation and especially at the vexed question
of homosexuality in the Church.

REMEMBERING

Remembering is highly personal. We remember the same events
differently and we may remember the same event with different
emphases depending on how we feel at the time we are

remembering. A joyous memory may have us laughing gently to ourselves or, in times of renewed grief, may have us in tears – 'There is no greater pain than to remember a happy event when one is in misery.'[3] Corporate remembering too can be selective and coloured by the present. History is written and re-written as the meaning attached to certain events is re-interpreted, new insights are gained and time creates a wider space for reflection.

> Human memory is a marvellous but fallacious instrument ...
> The memories which lie within us are not carved in stone; not only do they tend to be erased as the years go by, but often they change, or even increase by incorporating extraneous features ...[4]

However many facts are available to us we are still open to the selective decisions of those who have recorded the facts and in reading about them we are open to the writer's interpretation. History both reveals and conceals in order to present a view, an interpretation, meaning and order out of what might have been chaos.

Yet it is important that we remember those events in our personal and collective history that still have lessons for us. It is also important to allow the present its own voice – to break down barriers of prejudice, power, advantage, education, and wealth so that 'a whisper will be heard'.[5]

A WHISPER WILL BE HEARD

Dorothee Soelle, in her book *Suffering*, argues that:

> There are forms of suffering that reduce one to a silence in which no discourse is possible any longer, in which a person ceases acting as a human agent. Extreme external conditions such as exist in camps where people are starving or in destructive psychoses are examples of such senseless suffering. It is senseless because the people affected by it no longer have any possibility of determining a course of action, of learning from their experience, or of taking measures that would change anything... There are examples of suffering that lead to the abandonment of all hope for oneself... There is pain that renders people blind and deaf. Feeling for others dies: suffering isolates the person and he no longer cares about anyone but himself. Death becomes increasingly attractive ...[6]

It is impossible to express such extreme suffering in words, or even in cries. Pain is the entire landscape – an interminable, boundless, sameness of suffering. When a way is found to stand back slightly from that total captivity of pain it may be possible to begin to express it in sobs, in cries, in words, or in profound silence.

They had longed for this child – their first son though they had two daughters.

He was a happy baby and much loved. Their friends rejoiced with them. Then one morning she went to his room and found him dead.

Silence. No breathing.

No words, not even a cry would come to her lips.

Days later there was the funeral. The chapel was full to overflowing. A grave supportive silence filled the air. The minister found few words that could suffice. Much more was said in silent solidarity, in sensitivity to the parents' own convictions and beliefs, in being able to make possible a ceremony that would reflect the pain and yet bring hope.

After the service the parents led the way out to the cemetery garden. Friends came past, saying little – only a word here or there, but gentle hugs, embraces, touch said all. Then people stood in the sunlight in silence. The pain was too great for words. And then came the sound of weeping and one person's tears evoked another's. It was some time later that tears gave way to words.

If we are to use suffering we need to allow it to find its voice. Then we can allow it to inform our consciousness and teach us its wisdom. It may even be that the place of suffering is the place of divine encounter.

> . . . Awareness of God does not come by degrees:
> from timidity to intellectual temerity;
>> from guesswork, reluctance, to certainty;
> it is not a decision reached at the crossroads of doubt.
> It comes when, drifting in the wilderness,
>> having gone astray,
> we suddenly behold the immutable polar star.
> Out of endless anxiety,
> out of denial and despair,
> the soul bursts out in speechless crying.[7]

JANUARY 27TH

On January 27 1945, Auschwitz was 'liberated'. It is a date on which to remember all those who died at the hands of Nazism.

> Between five and six million Jews... perished in National Socialism's program of population elimination... The total more than doubles when one notes non-Jewish statistics such as the following: 3.3 million Soviet POWs perished in Nazi captivity; more than four million Soviet civilians, over 2.5 million Polish civilians, and 1.5 million Yugoslav civilians met similar fates. It should also be noted that up to five hundred thousand of Europe's seven hundred thousand Gypsies were slaughtered. In addition to German citizens who lost their lives in the euthanasia campaign, another thirty two thousand were executed between 1933 and 1945 for political crimes. Thousands of homosexuals, singled out as 'defectives' were eradicated. With a vengeance, the Nazi ideology of racial purity rendered people unwanted.[8]

Why should we want to go on remembering such an atrocity? Herman Wouk makes the point that, 'The beginning of the end of War lies in Remembrance'.[9] In another context George Santayana says, 'Those who cannot remember the past are condemned to repeat it'.[10] Remembering, learning about the past and trying to learn from it lies at the heart of creating a hopeful future. It is in this way that we may use even senseless suffering and may truly honour the dead.

> ... But the past is just the same, – and War's a bloody game ...
> have you forgotten yet? ...
> Look down and swear by the slain of the War that you'll
> never forget.
>
> Do you remember the dark months you held the sector at
> Mametz, –
> The nights you watched and wired and dug and piled
> sandbags on parapets?
> Do you remember the rats; and the stench.
> Of corpses rotting in front of the front line trench, –
> And dawn coming, dirty white, and chill with a hopeless rain?
> Do you ever stop and ask 'Is it all going to happen again?'.[11]

Sassoon's words remind us to remember. Perhaps they also foreshadow his own life. He spoke of 'my queer craving to revisit the past and give the modern world the slip.'[12] There is in this remembering the danger of not engaging fully with the present, not letting go of the past, not making a choice for life *now*.

IT'S NOT MY FAULT IF I LIVE AND BREATHE[13]

These words were written by Primo Levi. Born in Turin in 1919, Levi trained as a chemist. During World War II he fled to the mountains and formed a partisan band. At the end of 1943 he was captured and sent to a detention centre at Fossoli. In February 1944 he was taken to Auschwitz and was an inmate there until its 'liberation' in 1945. Those ten months haunted the rest of his life. He saw his raison d'être as having its root in the camp:

> The need to tell the story to 'the rest', to make 'the rest' participate in it, had taken on for us, before our liberation and after, the character of an immediate and violent impulse, to the point of competing with other elementary needs.[14]

He writes, 'to satisfy this need; first and foremost as an interior liberation'[15], but he also recognises that 'We the survivors, are not the true witnesses.'[16]

> The 'true witnesses' – those, that is, in full possession of the terrible truth – are the *sommersi*: the drowned, the submerged, the annihilated. They were not merely destroyed they were blotted out of existence.[17]

So Levi writes, 'We speak in their stead, by proxy.'[18] He speaks from his own experience and his own guilt at having survived:

> It's not my fault if I live and breathe,
> Eat, drink, sleep and put on clothes.[19]

Here is a man who suffered his own suffering as well as his share in the suffering of his people. His cry was a cry for humanity – 'I cannot tolerate the fact that a man should be judged not for what he is but because of the group to which he happens to belong...' It was also a cry to learn from the past. Paul Bailey, in his introduction to Levi's book *The Drowned and the Saved*, writes 'A would-be tyrant is waiting in the wings, with 'beautiful words' on his lips. The book is constantly impressing upon us to learn from the past, to make sense of the senselessness'.[20]

Few witnesses to the Holocaust surpass Levi in using suffering to discover great wisdom and humanity and in communicating those things in his writing.

Those who seek to bear witness are sometimes accused of wallowing in suffering. Elie Wiesel, another survivor of the Holocaust, responds:

> with a phrase borrowed from the writer Manes Sperber, who in turn had paraphrased a Talmudic saying. Even if I wrote on nothing else, it would never be enough, even if all the survivors did nothing but write about their experiences, it would still not be enough.[21]

Wiesel speaks of the importance of remembering:

> Remembering means to shed a merciless light on faces and events, to say 'No' to the sands that bury faces and words, and to forgetfulness and death.

> Of course, I could write my memories of the camp, which I bore within me like a poison . . . I thought about it with apprehension day and night; the duty to testify, to offer depositions for history, to serve memory . . . Memory is a passion no less powerful or pervasive than love. What does it mean to remember? It means to live in more than one world, to prevent the past from fading and to call upon the future to illuminate it.

This rationale suggests that the experience of intense suffering marks one for life. It wounds the core of one's being. It simply *cannot* be forgotten. It is only a word away from consciousness. When we can learn to remember wisely and let suffering teach us its wisdom, such remembering is constructive and drives us to fuller life.

> A Jew considers pain an insult to man. I have no right to turn my back on the suffering of others. Jews must 'choose life', in the here and now, and the living. In fact the same word – *hayyim* – means both 'life' and 'the living'.[22]

Choosing life, looking to the future, and remembering the past are not opposites. They are to be held together – 'Remembrance of what has been endured summons the future'[23] – and remembering the dead means that their death is not in vain. It means that we can use their suffering:

Doesn't all remembering of them (the dead) and all praying for them, all eating in remembrance of them have this character, that we 'need' the dead in a double sense, of wanting them and of making use of them? They have been taken from us and are unable to prevent this use of themselves. But *there is no way for us to love them other than to incorporate them into our work at living.*[24] (my italics).

This affirms their and our humanity. Perhaps it lies at the heart of using suffering in the service of life.

APARTHEID

Levi's comment, 'I cannot tolerate the fact that a man should be judged, not for what he is but because of the group to which he happens to belong . . .' can be applied to many situations of suffering including that of racism. Racial health, or what Alice Walker has called, 'a sense of Black people as complete, complex, *undiminished* human beings'[25] demands that each person has their own voice, their own integrity.

It demands that we refuse to be made less than human by others. One of the most telling phrases from Desmond Tutu's account of the Truth and Reconciliation Commission in South Africa is from a priest who said of those who tortured him, 'These are God's children and yet they are behaving like animals. They need us to help them recover the humanity they have lost.'[26]

To remember the past wisely, to listen well to the voices of the voiceless in our own generation is to enable others and ourselves to recover our humanity.

SUFFERING MAY REDUCE US TO NOTHING

Suddenly this professional woman who seemed so strong, so capable became silent. What was it that had reminded her of her childhood? What had triggered the memory of being abused by her father? She couldn't say. All she could say was it always took her back to the same feeling – that she was 'nothing'. Her head told her otherwise but caught in the grip of the memory her head struggled for mastery.

The woman's story is the story of all who have suffered greatly and have been victims of others. Desmond Tutu speaks of black people in South Africa before the end of apartheid who had been 'turned into the anonymous ones – faceless, voiceless, counting for nothing in their motherland'[27] . . .' they were invisible in the land of their birth.'[28]. Primo Levi too speaks of being reduced to nothing:

> Then for the first time we became aware that our language lacks words to express this offence, the demolition of a man[29]. . . the resolution of others to annihilate us first as men in order to kill us more slowly afterwards.[30]

Against such inhumanity suffering can strengthen our resolve to affirm humanity in whatever ways we can, to make visible those who have been conditioned to make themselves invisible.

LIVING THE TRUTH

There are no ways in which we can put suffering on the scales and see whether one suffering is greater, more noble, than another. Perhaps the clearest way of looking at suffering is that suggested by Dorothee Soelle, who was influenced by Paul Tillich:

> I would like to distinguish this meaningless suffering from suffering that can be meaningful since it impels one to act and thereby produces change.[31]

The rest of this chapter seeks to look at the issue of homosexuality in the Christian Church as a form of suffering that could impel the church to act and produce change. It is the suffering of those who are invited to live lives of pretence and deny their reality for the sake of the church.

> The Church has always been willing to receive the gifts of its gay priests, but it has seldom been willing to acknowledge with honesty their presence or to affirm their being . . . The Church's word to homosexual people is forthright: You cannot be who you are. You must, therefore, pretend to be who you are not. That is the price of survival in this institution.[32]

Of a priest his partner writes:

> So long as Barry's sexuality was invisible, it wasn't real. And if unreal, then it presented no obstacle to a life in the church. Such was the faulty reasoning . . .[33] But it's costing us too much, hiding our love, hiding who we are.[34]

This sense of the need to be invisible is well attested in gay literature:

> Gay men present an interesting anomaly in the construction of sexuality and gender in society. We are *visible* as men and thus linked to dominant systems of patriarchal power but only in so far as our sexuality is kept *invisible*. Once seen as gay we quickly become identified with the marginalised, the other. This complex dynamic of both incorporation by and alienation from society frames the development of a gay man's world view.[35]

INVISIBILITY

This invisibility is one of the marks of inhumanity whether it affects women, the mentally ill, those in residential care, the disabled or lesbians and gay men. What we wish to be invisible *we wish did not exist*. The desire that homosexuality should be invisible especially in the Church is reflected often in homosexuals themselves. It is described well in a letter from a gay man to his mother. His parents have recently written to him of the 'problem' of homosexuals. Having not 'come out' to them, he now writes them this letter:

Dear Mama,

I am sorry it has taken me so long to write. Every time I try . . . I realise I'm not saying the things that are in my heart. That would be OK if I loved you any less than I do, but you are still my parents and I am still your child . . .

I wouldn't have written, I guess, if you hadn't told me about your involvement in the Save Our Children campaign. That, more than anything, made it clear that my responsibility was to tell you the truth, that your own child is homosexual, and that I never needed saving from anything except the cruel and ignorant piety of people like Anita Bryant.

I'm sorry, Mama, not for what I am, but for how you must feel at this moment. I know what that feeling is, for I felt it for most of my life. Revulsion, shame, disbelief – rejection through fear of something I knew, even as a child, was as basic to my nature as the color of my eyes.

No, Mama, I wasn't recruited. No seasoned homosexual served as my mentor. But you know what? I wish someone had. I wish someone older than me and wiser than the people of Orlando had taken me aside and said, 'You're all right kid . . .

You're not crazy or sick or evil. . . . Most of all though, you can love and be loved without hating yourself for it.' But no one ever said that to me, Mama. I know what you are thinking right now – you're asking yourself, 'What did we do wrong? . . . Which one of us made him that way?'

. . . All I know is this: If you and Papa are responsible for the way I am then I thank you with all my heart for it's the light and the joy of my life.

It's not hiding behind words, Mama . . . It's not fearing your body . . . It's not judging your neighbour . . . Being gay has taught me tolerance, compassion and humility. It has shown me the limitless possibilities of living. It has given me people whose passion and kindness and sensitivity have provided a constant source of strength.

It has brought me into the family of man, Mama, and I like it here. I like it. Please don't feel you have to answer this right away. It is enough for me to know that I no longer have to lie to the people who taught me to value the truth. . .

Your loving son,
Michael[36]

I NO LONGER HAVE TO LIE TO THE PEOPLE WHO TAUGHT ME TO VALUE THE TRUTH

Here lies the crunch for the Christian who is also gay. The very institution which witnesses to the truth that will set us free invites some of its members not to be truthful about themselves, even to themselves. Whilst theological and Biblical points are scored, inhumanity continues.

For thirty years he had been faithful to what he thought was required of him by God, the Church and his family.

It was built into him that to be gay and a priest was not possible. He didn't need the homophobia of others. He had internalised it early on. So he had been faithful to his marriage and tried to kill off the part of himself that so yearned for expression.

Of course, in killing off that part of himself he was actually reducing his hold on life. He was committing himself to a life of pretence though the consciousness of that commitment, that choice, did not emerge until much, much later. For much of his life his homosexuality was like a shadow at the back of his mind. Now and again the shadow would obscure his thinking and feeling and he would turn away not knowing what to do with it.

The cost which he thought he carried alone was inflicted on others too. Like an explosive device waiting to go off, his anguish would emerge in all sorts of ways. People could see the struggle in his eyes, the strain in his face.

In the end it came to divorce. He was still faithful – 46 and never touched a man, never expressed the physicality of his being in what was for him the most natural way.

Divorce eased the pressure but made more apparent the prison that his perception of the church had become for him. The church required of him officially celibacy, but unofficially hiddenness and pretence – a fatal collusion for one who valued integrity.

It was reducing him to nothing. He who had struggled so long to affirm his humanity now felt more strongly than ever his humanity denied.

Thomas Merton wrote on a similar theme:

> For me to be a saint means to be myself. Therefore the problem of sanctity and salvation is in fact the problem of finding out who I am and of discovering my true self.
>
> ... God leaves us free to be whatever we like. We can be ourselves or not as we please. We are at liberty to be real or unreal. We may be true or false, the choice is ours. We may wear now one mask and now another, and never, if we so desire appear with our own true face.

But he gives a warning:

> we cannot make these choices with impunity. Causes have effects, and if we lie to ourselves and to others, then we cannot expect to find truth ... If we have chosen the way of falsity we must not be surprised that truth eludes us when we finally come to need it.[37]

What happens when the Church itself, or sections of it, condemn what we are out of hand and when even those who are sympathetic will invite duplicity and invisibility as the way of dealing with who we are?

When the powerful require others to be invisible this indicates that they see them as less than themselves and sometimes less than human. It is not enough to claim acceptance of the right to be homosexual but refuse to accept that gay men and women live in committed relationships, just as heterosexuals do.

> Our sexuality is an indivisible part of our humanity. To ask us, regardless of our sexual orientation, to deny and reject our sexuality – who we fantasise about, who we desire, who we fall in love with, who we love – is to ask us to split ourselves away from the most fundamental part of our being, the place which is at the centre of our humanity, from which all longing, desire, passion and creativity emerges.[38]

OPPRESSION BY STRUCTURES

The churches' attitude to homosexuality is a microcosm of the whole system of oppression – a system encapsulated by Kathleen Fischer:

> In any relationship where one individual or group is dominant and another is subordinate, the dominant group tends to act in certain typical ways. This is true whether the power inequality flows from gender, race, class, or other considerations. The individual or group in power: (1) tends to act destructively to subordinate groups; (2) restricts the subordinate group's range of action, even reactions to this destructive treatment; (3) discourages the subordinates' full and free expression of their experience; (4) characterises subordinates falsely; and (5) describes all this as the way it should be, usually as ordered and ordained by higher and better powers, ranging from biology to God.[39]

This final point is perhaps the most difficult to bear since the oppressor places responsibility on God rather than taking responsibility for the effects of their beliefs and actions. It can turn into a sophisticated and theological, but in some ways arbitrary game in which we can choose to use God to castigate those who do not live according to accepted value systems.

A few verses of scripture can be used – not as God's word which seeks to draw us to himself in justice and love – but as weapons to separate us. So often the wider demands of the gospel are rejected for the sake of a narrow and limited rationale. (Matthew 23: 23) Ultimately our understanding of the nature of God as revealed in Christ comes into question. What beliefs are provisional and open to change and what are fundamental?

STRUCTURAL BELIEFS

Jonathan Glover writes of 'structural beliefs':

> Some beliefs are about the acceptability of other beliefs, and are
> used to adjudicate between them. They could be called struc-
> tural beliefs. They are like the load bearing walls of a house.[40]

We are often divided by our structural beliefs. If we take human
values such as respect for the individual and realistic sympathy as
central to an understanding of our approach to another; if we place
Jesus' emphasis on justice, love, trust, forgiveness and compassion
as structural beliefs in our approach to God, others and ourselves,
then we will approach relationships with this basic structure of
beliefs and attitudes. If, on the other hand, we take marriage as a
structural belief rather than a derivative belief we regard marriage
alone as the adult way of relating wholly. This leaves many,
including the gay community, feeling second-class and excluded.

It's been said that the only way for change to happen is if 'the
strong Evangelical community can be convinced that scripture is
pointing in that direction'.[41] If structural beliefs play a part in change
then what is required is not just theological argument but transformed imaginations. As Jonathan Glover says, 'A code of Ethics
for officials should include having the imagination to look through
the rules to the human reality'. 'Real cultivation of the moral imagination is a threat to many comforting conventional attitudes.'[42] For
the church, structural beliefs need to be defined by God's view of
humanity, not by allowing humanity to be defined by unquestioned
structural beliefs. To take this risk is not to devalue marriage. It is
to value it more highly by recognising the importance of each individual within it. It also respects those who find marriage either
impossible or undesirable.[43]

ARTICULATING THE PAIN

Homosexuality is only one issue affecting the church where it is
hard not to feel that unless you meet certain criteria you are second-
class. It is hard to reconcile with a Lord who ate with tax collectors
and sinners and who listened to their voices as well as calling them
to live by values of the kingdom. Many Christians will have been
affected by the 1998 Lambeth Conference debate on sexuality. For
those Christians who happen to be homosexual it was another

example of fear dominating a Christian assembly, of rejection *before* an offer to listen.

Meanwhile, many feel diminished as people and having to live double lives without the freedom to explore relationships in an open and accepting way. Desmond Tutu says of apartheid that it 'succeeded only too well in dehumanising both those who implemented it and its victims'.[44] The same can be said of the churches' attitude to gay men and women. This is not to compare the levels of suffering involved. It is simply to articulate the suffering and to recognise that the greatest crime against another person is to fail to recognise their full humanity – a crime well documented and attested in the twentieth century from which there are lessons to be learnt.

REMEMBERING THE PAST AND PRESENT

Both the past and the present need to be brought to mind if we are to step wisely into the future. At best, remembering nourishes us with the blessing of the past. In the Jewish tradition and in the Eucharist it brings those blessings to the here and now. Remembering also brings to mind the pain and suffering of the past so that we might learn from it. To learn from it, to remember well, is to remember without judging. It is not to feel pressured into a forgiveness which cannot yet be given. It is simply to let the events unfold in our minds and be ready to gain new insight, fresh learning. It is to have compassion for ourselves and on others, but not to pretend.

The present needs to be heard well before it is judged. Reflection on events more often than not makes for better choices, better decisions, a better future.

THERE IS 'NO FUTURE WITHOUT FORGIVENESS'

The title of Desmond Tutu's book says it all. Remembering well must be done in the hope of forgiving well, but forgiveness is all too easily suggested to people before they are ready:

> Forgiving and reconciling are not about pretending that things are other than they are. It is not patting each other on the back and turning a blind eye to the wrong. True reconciliation exposes the awfulness, the abuse, the pain, the degradation, the truth. It could even sometimes make things worse. It is a risky undertaking, but in the end it is worthwhile, because in the end

there will be real healing from having dealt with the real situation. Spurious reconciliation can bring only spurious healing.[45]

Whether we are remembering our own personal history or the history of our peoples we know that what we do today may be rooted in the past – roots of love, self giving, and justice and roots of pain, resentment and inhumanity. Our present life will expose some of those roots. They will either become healed or like the exposed roots of a tree in a forest, continue to be something we and others may continually trip over.

As far we can we need to deal with those memories that imprison our lives if we are to make use of the suffering that they represent. We need to recognise that those memories which are so painful that they threaten to dominate us are not the whole story. Memories are like fish that swim in the underwater currents of our unconscious. Now and again they come to the surface unbidden and catch us by surprise by their swift liveliness and their shining clarity. At other times they linger just below the surface, elusive and mystifying.

At times they are evoked by a familiar scene, an unexpected letter, a scent or smell, a chance meeting. At other times we consciously draw them up by casting bait upon the surface of our mind and hoping to bring back into consciousness particular incidents in our lives like fish emerging from under the lily leaves. We want them to entertain us, to inform us, to clarify the meaning of the past and help us plan our future.

Memories are powerful but they can also be deceptive as we repress memories too painful to bear or highlight chosen memories which on their own may distort the true picture.

In fact we are not limited by our memories. Our minds are the stream in which they swim and if we want the whole picture of ourselves we need to consider not only our memories but to feel the flow of our lives – that flow which gives our life direction, which reminds us that we are still becoming and leads us to an eternal home in God.

FORGIVENESS

What then of forgiveness? The prophet Hosea emphasises 'hesed', God's covenanted love.

This may lead us to a definition of forgiveness as 'God's steadfast love reaching beyond all division' – the arms of Christ reaching out to draw all people to himself. You can almost feel the movement. It is a reaching out of self to the other. Forgiveness is reaching out beyond the divisions that have been created. This love, if it is true, doesn't encourage us to close in on ourselves, settling for a constant fingering of our wounds. We are not asked to make ourselves victims of further inappropriate wounding. This love allows us to come to a realistic appraisal of our life and still be open to love.

Forgiveness reaches beyond itself, gives itself in love. But forgiveness is not necessarily forgetting. When we forgive somebody who has hurt us we may need to remember what they have done as part of who they are. Otherwise our love for them is not embracing their reality. And to forgive is not to excuse what somebody has done, nor to say that we will be victim to their action again. It is to say that love has reached beyond it, as Christ even from the cross reached out in love to forgive.

Rowan Williams writes:

> The occasions when we feel genuinely forgiven are the moments when we feel, not that someone doesn't care what we do, but that someone *does* care what we do because he or she loves us and that that love is strong enough to cope with and survive the hurt that we have done'.[46]

God forgives us in this way. God acknowledges what has happened and moves beyond it. It is not dismissive. It is redemptive, based on reality, creating new depths and possibilities in all our relationships.

The alternative of living without forgiveness is to make a prison for ourselves and for others. Forgiveness is paramount in keeping love alive, paramount in keeping life loving. It is said of Brian Keenan, held hostage in Beirut, that he is compassionate rather than bitter and has an enormous capacity to love. 'What would be the point of staying bitter?' he asks, 'it would be as if I was still in captivity'. Captivity is a good word. Unforgiveness is its own captivity. Forgiveness is setting free ourselves and others. But forgiveness is costly. There is a cost for God and a cost for us and sometimes it can seem completely impossible – and we cannot judge others for that. Only victims of racism, prejudice, physical or emotional violence, rape, holocaust and genocide know what they have suffered. Nobody can forgive on their behalf, nor can they forgive until they have come to terms with themselves and what has happened to them. For those who believe, there is hope in the knowledge that God can forgive what we cannot and that God who suffers with us in our pain is also a victim of it. Forgiveness is a divine prerogative which we too are graced to share.

REMEMBERING WELL

In this chapter we have looked at the question of remembering and of the need to remember if we are to learn from the past. We have emphasised the need to listen to the 'invisible' ones and to hear their voice. Whether we are remembering the past or listening to the voices of the present we need to remember – to bring them to mind well – in an attitude of understanding love, not of closed minds. We have recognised the importance of forgiveness as a realistic and necessary task if our memories are to have constructive rather than destructive power.

This chapter has underlined too the need to use the present to shape our understanding and to clarify our 'structural beliefs'.

5

SUFFERING AND ISOLATION

I bid you but be;
> I have not need of prayer;
> I have need of you free
>> As your mouths of mine air;
That my heart may be greater within me, beholding the
fruits of me fair.

O my sons, O too dutiful
> Towards Gods not of me,
Was not I enough beautiful?
> Was it hard to be free?
For behold, I am with you, am in you and of you: look
forth now and see.[1]

Swinburne's poem reminds us of God's desire that we be free. The whole spiritual journey is a journey from slavery to freedom and needs to find expression in the whole of our lives. This freedom is dedicated to God, to all that is ultimately life-giving rather than death-dealing.

It hardly needs saying that suffering, especially extreme suffering, isolates. In this chapter we look at that isolation and at the positive and negative sides of being an individual. We look at ways of using isolation and ways of breaking free from its destruction. Finally we embrace the reality that some people find it impossible to break free except by bringing their own life to an end.

It is a hard-won freedom that takes us from the security of slavery to the risks of being free people, having to make choices and be fully responsible. To risk that freedom is to risk being truly ourselves. Sometimes it is a freedom which we seek. Sometimes it is a freedom that seeks us, maybe through the most painful of circumstances.

He had carried the secret of his life for long enough. Admitting it would change everything. He had been driven to the edge. In tears of desperation he heard himself saying again and again to a friend, 'I can't pretend any longer ...'

For him it was the beginning of a long period of coming to terms with the reality of his being and of allowing his outer life to be true to his inner. The journey for him from slavery to freedom would take resolve and courage and friends who could affirm him despite the pain that such a journey would involve.

Brian Keenan says of the freedom he found in his captivity, 'Captivity had re-created freedom for us. Not a freedom outside us to be hungered after, but another kind of freedom which we found to our surprise and relish within ourselves'. It is this inner freedom which may sustain us through times of suffering. It is this inner freedom that may allow us to make choices that create a greater outer freedom for ourselves and for others. It means coming to terms with ourselves in such a way that we free ourselves to be open to change and growth. As Carl Rogers says, 'we cannot change, we cannot move away from what we are, until we thoroughly *accept* what we are.'[2] This requires an acceptance of reality and an acceptance of suffering. 'Every acceptance of suffering is an acceptance of that which exists.'[3] Soelle reminds us that, 'It is paradoxical but true that unconditional love for reality does not in the least defuse passionate desires to change reality.'[4]

In suggesting that we accept reality we are not encouraging a fatalistic attitude towards it, but one of hope of change. In this light we may explore the experience of isolation.

DECREASING CIRCLES

We have already seen how affliction may cause people to become more distant and how any suffering has the potential to isolate. Such isolation may be exacerbated by the person's interior isolation from the world, especially people suffering mental illness[5] or the effects of serious trauma.

Less obvious suffering borne over a long period isolates too and often – the circle of friends and family becomes smaller and smaller.

A woman I know lives in a little Bavarian village with her husband and their three children. Her husband is a weak individual, small in stature and short on intellectual gifts. He has been drinking for many years, and when he comes home he kicks up a fierce storm, taking revenge on his wife for everything life withheld from him. He torments her incessantly. He accuses her of being a whore, yelling by the open window so that the neighbours hear it, waking the children. Often he beats her. She has no life of her own. She is never allowed to undertake anything independently and has no control over time or money. He also tries to take away the support her own family gives her, maligning her before her brothers and sisters.[6]

One can imagine how she (falsely) tries to protect her husband and family, trying to be faithful to a marriage that is no marriage. One can imagine how she questions herself as to what she has done to make him like this. She may easily become someone who fabricates the truth so much, not only to others but also to herself, that she can no longer see the truth of the situation, or act from it. Her isolation increases as she becomes alienated from herself. Of course isolation is not always a negative experience. It can be a place not of evasive falsehood but where new truth can confront and pierce us. If accepted, it can lead to more of our healing. The impact of truth in our isolation is challenging but also an impetus for real growth. Isolation then becomes solitude and aloneness, all-one-ness.[7]

INDIVIDUALISM, ISOLATION, SOLITUDE

In 1835 Alexis de Tocqueville, writing in *Democracy in America*, said of individualism that it is:

> . . . a calm and considered feeling which disposes each citizen to isolate himself from the mass of his fellows and withdraw into the circle of family and friends; with this little society formed to his taste, he gladly leaves the greater society to look after itself . . . Each man is forever thrown back on himself alone, and there is danger that he may be shut up in the solitude of his own heart.[8]

Suffering itself may enforce this individualism to an extreme degree where the person who is suffering gets lost in the pain, unable to reach out to others, concerned only for self and even then tempted to end it all rather than live with the intolerable landscape of emptiness and pain. This isolation reduces the person to silence, makes hope elusive and the ability to change the situation almost impossible. It is a condition of losing one's sense of humanity. It is an affliction which causes others to turn away not knowing how to respond – except for those who have the insight to carry on trying.

She tried to describe to him how he had been at his worst. It was almost impossible to find the words. He had suffered so long and from so many causes. As a friend she had always tried to be there for him even in the darkness but there were times she said when he simply wasn't there – when his selfhood seemed to disappear under the burden of suffering, times when she could not reach him, could not entice him to communicate. But she never gave up trying and more than anything her friendship pulled him through.

If we pursue the kind of individualism that de Tocqueville describes when things are going well, the more isolated we become when suffering comes upon us.

Coming to a healthy solitude is different from suffering in isolation. Sara Maitland describes one aspect of it in her novel *Virgin Territory*:

> There is no cheating yourself . . . If you loved yourself, all of yourself, in the dark corners and the tortured dreams and the dirty bits which are without words, without names, which were forgotten when the sweet brooding dove called all things out of chaos, if you loved yourself down into the darkness, you could love me too, because that is where I am and who I am.[9]

Loving ourselves 'in the dark corners' is part of the way to solitude but it can be a very long and wearying journey, perhaps only possible when one can believe in something or someone greater than oneself that offers compassion and forgiveness. That may be a friend or a professional therapist. Ultimately, for those who believe in a loving God, the one who loves our darkness into life is God himself.

> . . . as we look into the darkness that is *our* humanity (not a fiction, and not someone else's) we shall, the gospel tells us, meet that compassion that takes us through this darkness into the life of Christ, the forgiveness that establishes us in love and freedom. . .[10]

In the place of suffering we have to face not only the darkness but also pain and allow that pain to be touched by God. And it is *our* pain and *our* darkness that we need to address. It's too easy to tell ourselves that our suffering is minor in the face of other suffering –

that we should ignore ours in order to be concerned for others. At one level it is commendable but at another can be deeply damaging, for unless we accept the reality of our own life we will by our avoidance work it out in others rather than in ourselves. We need to accept responsibility for what is happening to us *as part* of our reaching out to others. By acknowledging the reality of our own experience, by giving it value, we also value others; by affirming our humanity, we affirm the humanity of others.

It is too easy to keep our suffering at the borders of our mind, never actually facing it and so never allowing it to be transformed, never allowing it to be put at the service of others.

She did not know how to begin to tell her story. She felt so ashamed. Here she was, a seemingly mature woman, and yet unable to come to terms with patterns that had become ingrained in childhood – patterns of feeling a disappointment to her parents, of never measuring up to expectations. So while others saw in her a capable and very gifted person she knew herself to be a needy and vulnerable child. The pain was immense, taking her sometimes to thoughts of suicide. But to feel what she felt was for her to admit herself a failure again – to feel like a wimp. 'I shouldn't feel like this . . . I oughtn't still be feeling these things . . . others have suffered more than me.'

He listened, full of compassion, knowing that what he heard was precious and valuable and, quite contrary to her expectations, made him respect her more, not less, for here was someone daring to let their pain move from the fringes of their life to the centre.

THE CENTRE AS THE PLACE OF TRANSFORMATION

The movement of experience from the fringes to the centre of our awareness is often the movement that causes us to act on that experience. We may go for years knowing that we are not dealing with what is true for us. Then something happens which brings that awareness to the centre. We experience our truth. For some of us that awareness will also be an awareness of God.

It is necessary for us to take pain and disappointment into the centre of our experience precisely because they are in the centre of God's experience. Suffering does not lie on the fringes of God's awareness, but at the core . . . God embraces suffering and makes it his own.[11]

. . . progress in life – if we are earnest and reflective – is marked by the shifting of sorrows and joys from the outer fringes of our experience and our calculations to the centre of our realisation of life (a personal encounter) and to the centre of our picture of life (an intellectual construction).[12]

This movement from the fringes to the centre may lessen suffering's hold on us and empower us to articulate and then act upon what we learn from it. Suffering can so often be our teacher. Indeed in some instances it will be the only teacher we have if we are prepared to listen.

He'd gone to a therapist expecting some illumination on what was happening in his life, longing to discover ways of coming to terms with the depression that dogged him. He wanted to get away from it, be freed of its treacly grasp. He was surprised then when the therapist said to him, 'This depression is your friend. What is it trying to tell you?' At first he was angry. Depression was no friend. It had almost made an end of him. But later, reflecting, he realised that the depression was making him face up to things he had long avoided.

When he saw the therapist again, he could begin to address those issues.

THE PAIN OF ISOLATION

Again and again we need to remind ourselves that extreme pain, intense suffering does not permit the kind of reflection that this man was enabled to do. It may completely lock a person in its grasp, making survival itself the only concern. The pain can be physical, resulting in extreme situations in an animal scream. There is also the less obvious tyranny of one's own mind and heart, which may also have us screaming. Thomas Mann writes:

> Solitude gives birth to the original in us, to beauty unfamiliar and perilous – to poetry. But it also gives birth to the opposite; to the perverse, the illicit, the absurd.[13]

His words could almost be a summary of Brian Keenan's time in captivity. From that experience Keenan produced the most beautifully poetic book about his experience of incarceration but the book, though poetic, does not deny the horrors and especially the tyranny of the mind and the pain of suffering for oneself and for one's companions. He writes: 'Always in the darkness the mind finds free passage to the most awful places'.[14]

Primo Levi writes of a similar experience:

... but as soon as we close our eyes, once again we feel our brain start up, beyond our control; it knocks and hums, incapable of rest, it fabricates phantasms and terrible symbols, and without rest sharpens and projects their images, as a grey fog, on to the screen of our dreams.[15]

This torment is known by all who suffer greatly or who suffer in lesser ways over a long period so that suffering becomes like fading wallpaper which has become too familiar to change, until someone stops and looks at it. The need to hide one's sexuality is likely to cause this intense suffering at times.

Inside,
I am a screaming child –
my needs unmet.
I do not know how much longer
I can contain myself.
A boiling cauldron
waiting to explode,
implode –
the risk is high.

I know myself too well,
the signs I read
and desperately ignore –
the danger to my present life too high.

I have within a deep capacity to love
It comes from God
of that I have no doubt
But how to express?
It is not understood,
this love of man for man.

I am alone,
totally alone
or that is how it feels
and loneliness consumes
fulfils itself
and I am lost.

This intense pain wears a person down. It takes a conscious decision to maintain one's humanity in this wilderness of living.

THE WILDERNESS

Perhaps of all the images of spiritual life the wilderness is the most perverse. The wilderness is the place where we confront ourselves and God, nakedly facing the wild beasts of our existence. It can be a place of sublime encounter or of massive destruction. It is not a place to go by choice but only when we have no choice – when circumstances take us there – or when God calls us to enter the desert of our lives.

It is helpful perhaps to differentiate between a real and a false desert. A real desert is one where we face reality, where idols are smashed, where we are stripped of illusions and, in the spiritual tradition, one where we seek God above all else. The false desert is the desert we create for ourselves by trying to lead lives based on illusion and falsehood. One leads to life even through its pain; the other leads to spiritual death.

The desert is the place where we may enter our deepest centre and pass through that centre into God, the place where we may come to know ourselves so well that we can give ourselves with abandon. It is the desert which may lead us to a true mysticism based on crystal clear honesty with oneself and with God. So the desert becomes a place of revelation, encounter and transfiguration, though much of what happens in the desert happens in the soul and is beyond words.

> A desert is a place where life is very condensed. The roots of living things hold onto that last tear of water and the flower hoards its moisture by only appearing in early morning and late afternoon. Life in the desert is small but brilliant and most of what occurs goes on underground . . . Many of us have lived desert lives: very small on the surface, and enormous under the ground.[16]

The desert then is the place where we learn to be alone – to be all-one, provided the desert does not first consume us. Being stripped can feel enormously threatening and dangerous. It can feel as though there will be nothing left.

What is being destroyed is illusion, the false self – that self which we so painstakingly erect to protect ourselves from the wounds we fear may happen to us, or from the experience of feeling again the pain of the wounds of childhood and adolescence. Our false self is our 'image' that responds to the expectations of those around us.

This self is often afraid that it will be found out – 'What would people think if they knew me as I *really* am?'

Many people prefer to stay with the false self, opting for a steady conformity rather than the pain and risk of moving beyond it. Then, often through great pain or great joy, life gives them a jolt, raises new challenges and questions assumptions. The invitation is being made to go into the desert – to walk away from the false self and change life to let the real self be known, not only in the innermost heart but in daily choices, attitudes and affections. In a sense the desert is the cocoon, the place where the caterpillar breaks down into a yucky mush before being re-formed into a butterfly. In reality the real self is not a new creation, but the emergence of the self that was created in God's love.

It is not something we create. It is the self we discover when illusion and falsehood have been burned away. There will be a collapse of all the games and pretence that kept the false self going. There will suffering in the process but there will also be a growing sense of integration and self-awareness to the extent of knowing that 'the only integration we can achieve in this life is the knowledge that we cannot achieve integration and the fullest maturity is to know our immaturity.'[17]

This process may take a lifetime as we return again and again at deeper levels to deal with fragments of our lives that need compassionate embrace and healing. In other words the desert is the place of conversion, a place where breakdown becomes transformation, where dying gives way to life.

This process, although painful, is not necessarily brutal. Nor is it self-inflicted. We discover it is happening to us and may choose to give our consent. It is not digging around looking for areas of pain in our lives to 'deal' with them. It is questing after truth and reality in our lives and dealing with the pain that comes as a result. For those who have suffered greatly it may well be that a level of 'denial' and 'filtering' of pain may be necessary in order not to be overwhelmed. It is also important to find safe places where these areas of our lives can be articulated without judgement and with compassion.

TELLING OUR STORY

To use our suffering means first that we have to acknowledge its reality and that is often done by finding places where the pain can be put into words – where our story can be told. We need to tell our story either to empower us to carry on bearing suffering about which we can do nothing, or to change the circumstances which are causing our suffering. We need to be able to express our story in safe places, places of trust where we may find tenderness, compassion, joy, friendships.[18]

The people who will help us are those who 'will not accept pretension, but will gently and firmly confront you with your own blindness'[19], a friend or professional helper who 'awakens your life in order to free the wild possibilities within you.'[20] The aim of telling our story is not to avoid dealing with what concerns us – ceaselessly telling our story to different people as a way of avoiding the risks of change – but in order to let our pain move us to action. Articulation is often the first stage.

Telling our story can also help us live with pain that we cannot change[21]. In part this is simply because telling our story to someone who listens well affirms our humanity. This is most evident in Desmond Tutu's account of the Truth and Reconciliation Commission in South Africa.

> Our nation sought to rehabilitate and affirm the dignity and humanity of those who were cruelly silenced for so long, turned into anonymous, marginalised victims. Now, through the Truth and Reconciliation Commission, they would be empowered to tell their stories, allowed to remember and in this public recounting their individuality and inalienable humanity would be acknowledged.[22]

Telling our story to another is often the way in which we establish trust. If we feel that they have listened well not just to the facts but to our feelings, that they understand and that they respect us, we are likely to trust them with ourselves. There are times when the quick development of such trust is crucial.[23]

Telling our story is important not only in terms of knowing that somebody has heard and affirmed us, but also for our own sake. It is often in recounting our experience that we recognise the significance, or lack of it, that we have given to its various aspects. Voicing our journey may be the way in which we interpret it in a different way and understand ourselves better.

Telling our story may be immensely draining of energy, especially when, for instance, a rape victim has to tell their story publicly in court. It may take us back into the pain. Some of the homosexuals who survived concentration camps were told, 'that it was over and done with and to leave the past in the past' and saw keeping their story to themselves as 'patiently bearing one's burden'. The makers of the first feature documentary telling their stories said of the men, 'No one has wanted to hear their stories for fifty years. They developed what inner resources they need to cope. Now when someone says we want to hear your story, it's not an opportunity they are going to jump at. It takes a lot of trust building.'[24] Inhumanity piled on inhumanity. It is possible to cause more pain if we try to drag stories out of people who are not yet ready or able to articulate them or if we are not the right person to hear them.

This choice of recipient for our story is important if the experience is to be healing. In the day-to-day encounters of life we present part of our story to all sorts of people. In doing so we discover our own identity, though we always risk misunderstanding, ignorance, prejudice and fear in the other.

It requires great trust to offer our greatest vulnerability to another and our story should not be wrested from us. Indeed it may well be that we need to explore our story with others before we can tell it even to ourselves. As Carter Heyward writes:

> . . . Our best protection is to speak the truth of our lives insofar as we can, with one another's presence and help, and cultivate carefully together those truths we cannot yet speak, truths that may be still very unformed and young.[25]

Some will tell their story not through words at all but as we have already seen through art, drama, cinematography, literature, dance and mime.

AND SOME WILL BE REDUCED TO A SCREAM

It doesn't happen now but for some time after my wife died I had only to think of that day and that moment and I could feel the scream inside myself. The word 'scream' is inadequate to describe the searing pain that nailed me to the spot and rendered me silent to others yet overwhelmed my senses.

I had nursed Jackie for five years and she had gradually lost the use of most of her body. She had lost the ability to physically care for her children, and her passion for art had been tested to the limits as she fought to keep painting despite her disability. It had become clear that now her lungs were affected badly. She had twice teetered on the edge of dying, brought back from the brink by oxygen and love. Her voice had been weak and there had often been times of frustration, humour and near hysteria as she tried to make herself understood. But this morning was different. It was clear that her death was imminent. She had been prepared in the way she wanted – washed, massaged, relaxed and ready – and then suddenly she could not speak at all. Somehow all the pain of the previous five years was condensed into that one moment and went through me as I watched. I had never known such pain – the pain of being alongside another's suffering.

Brian Keenan knows this scream in himself and in a fellow hostage:

> Then my idle pondering was abruptly brought to a halt. I heard what I had never heard before. A man crying out loud, the type of cry that tells you that a fierce blow has been laid upon him and then another and another cry. Then those cries of pain becoming screams of a kind of animal helplessness. These were not screams of fear but of pain. This was a man being tortured.[26]

> ... and then I heard it ... A noise that I have never heard before, nor since, nor do I ever want to hear it again. I know only that it came from me, yet it did not come from me. It was a cry so awful and so excruciating, which came from some part of me but was not willed by me. It was a primordial sound, fusing every moment of anguish in me. Where it came from I don't know, only that I was the vehicle through which it passed.[27]

AND SOME TO SILENCE

We shall explore the theme of silence more in chapter 11. There are times when suffering reduces us to silence and often to waiting when we know that at the present time we can do nothing about our suffering but bear it as patiently as we can, waiting for the 'right' time before we act or accepting that we cannot act. In the waiting time it may be that articulating our pain alleviates it to a degree, as I discovered for myself a few years ago in a poem

which receives further attention in Chapter 11. Or it may be that we
need to hold it silently.

> Holy God,
> Insubstantial one,
> feather on the breath of my being,
> let me cherish your presence.
>
> What had held me together,
> held no more.
> Meanings and explanations,
> understandings and passions
> all gone.
> Depression they called it.
> What a wimp of a word![28]
>
> Caged into my stillness,
> somnambulant rage[29]
> pinning me down.
> My inscape, a void.
> Pain glancing me,
> hardly perceived
> but still piercing.
> Why had it beaten me so,
> why cowered me into
> this overcast cave?
>
> And words which at first,
> could not touch me
> became, as I wakened, artillery fire –
> too much, too much to bear.
>
> My soul refuses all comfort
> yet needed you there.[30]
> Perverse in its longings
> yet knowing that
> walking, too soon, from the dark
> was not healing.
>
> And you, insubstantial one,
> whistling of a gentle air[31]
> drew me to wait in the darkness,
> in hell not despairing,[32]
> till freedom should come.

AND SOME TO SUICIDE

He'd always felt that the person he really was was not acceptable to others so his life had been an enormous effort to conform, to 'belong' though belonging seemed out of reach. As he came into his middle years – mid-life crisis would be too weak a description – he realised that his inner and outer worlds were dangerously polarised. To the world he was successful, capable, reliable. To himself he was lonely, empty, fearful and unsure. When family pressures began to dominate his life and his relationship was under strain he thought of suicide. It seemed the only way out. He could see no other. For nine months it taunted him – this apparent 'solution' to the insoluble, painful, depressing muddle of his life. Only the help of a pyscho-therapist and a good friend pulled him through – helped him see alternatives.

'It seemed the only way out'. The isolation of suffering comes to a potent vulnerability in someone who can see no way out of a situation or who is suffering from mental illness – someone who feels themselves already finished. 'Suicide, not because of conscious-ness of guilt but basically because I am already dead, draw a line . . .'[33]

We do well to listen to Father Zossima in Dostoevsky's *The Brothers Karamazov*:

> We are told that it is a sin to pray for them (those who have committed suicide) . . . but in my heart of hearts I think that we may pray even for them. *For Christ cannot be angry with love.* I have prayed inwardly all my life for such as those, I confess it to you, fathers and teachers, and I am still praying for them every day.[34] (my italics)

By such prayer those who have passed through the ultimate isolation may yet be surrounded by our love.

SUFFERING AND ISOLATION

Jesus' words that he is alone and not alone because the Father is with him (John 16: 32) are for us too and we may feel that it ought to be enough to know that God is with us even when we cannot feel his presence. In an incarnational religion however it is right to recognise the reality that isolation can be powerful and immensely destructive. In this chapter we have recognised the effect of isolation and affirmed the need for companionship and compassion – an area we will explore further in chapter 7.

6

CAUSING SUFFERING TO OTHERS

They were handsome men,
With blonde and red hair.
They were frightening,
They were arrogant,
They were German.

A woman watched,
A woman stared
At those arrogant ones,
Those handsome ones.

She watched them marching.
She watched and thought
Of her husband,
A prisoner in their country;
And she spat.

She was alone:
They were alone;
He was alone;
They were all prisoners,
Prisoners of war.[1]

This poem conveys how a young person looking back at war sees the interconnectedness of suffering. In Christianity such inter-relatedness is a strong theme.[2] In this chapter we look at how our own lives bring suffering to others – the pain we inflict on one another through ignorance, fear, being true to ourselves, being selfish and also through intentional and unintentional cruelty. We deal with the issue of failure and of the possibility of hope and trust.

INTERCONNECTEDNESS

Sharing our humanity happens at different levels. There are times when we are caught up in a crisis and are suddenly immersed in the suffering of another. At other times we may choose whether or not to be involved. At a deeper level we are involved in the suffering of humanity even when we make no such choice – we make our contribution to it as well as our contribution to relieve it.

When I was a child the north Norfolk coast was a favourite haunt (and still is). At that time the sewerage pipes could be seen going out to sea. The pollution was sometimes hidden from sight but at other times would come back onto the beach with the tide. Our contribution to society is much the same. Nobody else may be aware of the contribution, for good or ill, that we are making. Sometimes it remains hidden and unnoticed. At other times what we have given to society can come back with the tide and is brought to public attention. Our humanity or inhumanity affects the lives of others. Our connection with humanity is being worked out at deep levels. We are affecting and being affected by 'society'. We are projecting our aspirations and our fears, and 'society' projects its own onto us.

The image of the sewer is a graphic depiction of this deep truth[3] that we shape society and affect others and the wider world by our actions and by our attitudes.

The knowledge that we cause suffering to others can be a heavy burden. The task is to become aware without becoming over-whelmed. Indeed we may have had no choice. One daughter wrote of her mother's cancer, 'Disease may score a direct hit on only one member of the family, but shrapnel tears the flesh of the others. And as I had learned there was no quick way out of the war-zone.'[4]

This image is helpful in that it suggests how pain connects us, but becomes unhelpful if we see one person as the cause of pain. In the case of disease it is in fact the disease which has caused the explosion. In other situations one person may precipitate an 'explosion' but to attribute total responsibility without careful thought may be to impose an unbearable burden:

He was having difficulties in his marriage. Part of him wanted to walk away and begin life again. Another part of him longed to make the marriage work for the sake of the children. It felt as though he was being asked to give something which he did not have to give . . . if he couldn't find the resources in himself to carry on and if he couldn't live without hurting everybody perhaps it would be easier for everybody if he were not here. He felt trapped in a situation with few honourable ways out. Perhaps it was time to exit stage left – if only it could be done without hurting others.

In this extreme example the sense of being in the way by being oneself, coupled with a sense of seeing no way out, is a dangerous and isolating concoction. There is the burden of what one's action will do to others and at the same time recognition of the pain being caused to oneself by taking no action. Indeed, taking no action is a choice in itself. Underneath the despair is an assumption that it is possible not to cause pain to others. It simply isn't true. For this man it was not a matter of causing pain or not, but of recognising that pain was inevitable. Choices were possible only in terms of recognising that some pain would be less destructive than other. By moving towards taking the pain on himself – exiting stage left – he was not avoiding pain for others but risking unbearable pain for them.

In dealing with our life situation, then, the reality is that pain may be inevitable, and will certainly be unpredictable. It simply is not possible to predict how people will respond to any choice we make. Our imagination may wreak havoc as it gives the Hollywood treatment to any scenario we envisage. We may fear the worst and be pleasantly surprised, or hope for the best only to discover our hope was an illusion. That riskiness is part of the suffering but risk does not prevent us from going forward. Only fear does this. Risk does not relieve us of the need to choose life and take the risks that such a choice entails.

PROTECTING SELF AND OTHERS

Unless one accepts that pain is inevitable one is drawn to try to protect oneself and others from pain. At times this is possible and sensible but at other times it merely increases the isolation and deepens the pain. Its invisibility is only superficial. It will emerge often in destructive ways.

The girl was mystified. Something in the house had changed. Her parents were going about differently. Perhaps she had hurt them. She puzzled for a long time about how she might have done wrong. Evening after evening, coming home from school, she walked into an unsettling silence in the house. Comforting herself by hugging the dog, she would gently weep, not knowing the cause of her sadness nor of the painful silence. It was a year later that her parents plucked up the courage to tell her that her grand-fathers, who she seldom saw, had both died the year before – within three days of each other. Overcome by grief themselves the parents could not handle telling the girl. . . but the silence and the pain, the uncertainty and the unfocused guilt stayed with the girl into adulthood.

This incident highlights the question of whom we seek to protect when we protect others from pain. Sometimes it is right to protect others for their sake. But at other times we protect ourselves from seeing others' pain because we are unable to cope with it as well as our own.[5] Watching others in pain, especially those close to us, can cause another level of pain. This is true when one is a bystander and who can do nothing to help, but when one is the cause of another's pain there is another level of anguish on both sides. The person who causes the pain may also want to be the one who mitigates it – like a parent seeking to correct and then embrace a child – but finds that such attempts only deepen the agony.

Self awareness, honesty and facing reality help us to discern whether it is right to draw others into an awareness of pain. Discernment is necessary in considering who to tell, and when and how to tell them.

DENYING YOURSELF AND ANNIHILATING YOURSELF

The woman's life was a misery. Her husband kept most of his pay for himself, leaving only a small amount to feed and dress the family. She would sometimes argue with him but to no effect and in the end, for the sake of the children she kept quiet – 'anything to keep the peace'. It was destructive for her and for the children. They could sense the lack of respect between the parents, they experienced the shortage of cash, they saw how the husband spent his money – cigarettes, alcohol and gambling. Their respect for their mother was tinged with misunderstanding – for why did she let herself be so down-trodden? It was painful for them to watch. They could not bear the burden 'that it was for their sake'.

The gospel imperative to deny oneself and take up the cross daily (Luke 9: 23) can easily be converted into a self-annihilation which is far from God's intention and will. It is the difference between 'giving yourself' and 'giving yourself away', between self-giving and self-immolation.

Karl Barth says of God that he 'gives himself, but he does not give himself away.' Seen in this light 'taking up one's cross' takes on a new light. It is not denying our true selves. It is knowing ourselves to be valued and valuing ourselves, yet reaching beyond ourselves for the sake of others. It is a free choice, or at least a consent to the seemingly inevitable, rather than a destruction of self.

It is a self-respect that is generous both in self-giving and in a refusal to forsake one's own humanity even in desperate circumstances. To quote Karl Barth again: 'God gives himself, but he does not give himself away . . . He does not cease to be God.'[6]

DISCERNING A WAY FORWARD

If pain is inevitable and the suffering we experience in a situation is to be used, then we need to discern how best to handle the suffering that comes our way. We need to endeavour to be aware of the suffering we cause by our actions (but not paralysed by it) and discover how best to respond in our relationships with others. For the believer there is also the whole question of how we relate to God and how we experience his will. Religion can have a powerful effect, for good or ill, on the way that we deal with a situation.

He was paralysed by indecision. He and his wife had agreed long ago that their marriage was over. Indeed they had not lived together for many years and there had been unfaithfulness early on in the relationship. But when the question of divorce was raised he could not begin to address it for he was firmly convinced that divorce was wrong and that having made the vows in church they could not be broken. All the time his need for intimacy and companionship taunted him and from time to time he would begin a relationship but it would go nowhere for he could neither let go of his past nor take hold of his future.

In fact, he was fulfilling a sense of duty towards his children, though they had grown up, and fulfilling the role expectations of his parents and of his understanding of the church's teaching. But he was not fully consenting to either because he was not allowing himself to see that he had a choice. He could not commit himself either to the marriage or to moving on but wavered between the two, increasing the suffering and exhausting himself and others.

ROLE EXPECTATION AND DUTY

Often what is in question is the role we have tried to take upon ourselves in order to satisfy ourselves or others. Dorothee Soelle writes:

> To be caught up in one role, without flexibility, predisposes one to suffer. 'Alienation from one's self means a narrowing of role distance and thereby a suppression of necessary personal achievements in playing one's role. This occurs through unduly great pressure to conform to certain behaviour norms, a pressure that is expressed in narrow and overly precise role expectations.'[7] According to this view role-distance and diversity of roles would be recommended as ways of avoiding social suffering and suffering caused by society. The sufferer is 'no longer the master but the slave in his own role-household.'[8]

Such alienation from self causes great suffering not only to the individual but to those around them for the element of choice that is fundamental to our humanity is turned into a servant to an arbitrary yet powerful 'model' of what we or others think we should be. Scripturally there is one verse which can so easily be interpreted in this way: Matthew 5: 48, 'Be perfect, therefore, as your heavenly Father is perfect'. The idea of 'perfection' creates an illusion that we can make ourselves better by trying harder, by squeezing ourselves into an image of perfection which may be arbitrary, unattainable and damaging. Theologically such an attempt has no basis. We cannot make ourselves perfect. Only God can do that – it's his work of grace.

In fact the word translated as 'perfect' is more about being complete or finished (Gk. *telos*). On the cross Jesus said, 'It is finished' – a word he uses when to human eyes he is in the lowest place. Like a criminal he is fastened to a cross on the city's refuse heap. Nothing is perfect here but everything is complete. For Christ, being 'perfect' is not about self-protection.

For Jesus perfection is not about conforming to the demands of law or the expectations of others. It is about living the truth of his nature in all the circumstances in which he finds himself – not forcing himself but making himself *available* to God. Not perfect, but completely receptive, completely available. To live this way is not to be constrained by convention or pretence but to dare to live the truth. It is to challenge those who prefer outward observance to a manner of living which stems from inner fidelity to God's call. It is not a denial of duty but a fulfilment.

There are times when it is entirely appropriate to act 'in role'. A role can set us free to serve others in a way which is consistent and does not depend on our own response to another: for example, a teacher tries to respond even-handedly with pupils from different backgrounds. This is clearly necessary in a healthy society. But a role which has become so much a part of us that we no longer know our own self has become destructive and demands that we dare to step out of that role and find ourselves again.

DUTY, OBEDIENCE AND SELFHOOD

This raises the whole question of duty, obedience and selfhood. In chapter 5 we gave an example of how easy it was for the lady in the Bavarian village to, 'become someone who tells so many fabrications of the truth – not only to others but to oneself – that one can no longer see the truth of the situation, nor act from it.'[9] This is the key to the issue, especially when some of the fabrications are part of a belief system which is enforced upon us or which we have accepted uncritically. Duty, discipline and obedience are necessary in a healthy society but, precisely because we recognise that, they are open to manipulation and control by the unscrupulous or unthinking. Martin Israel makes the point that, 'It needs also to be said that our first duty is towards our own well-being, because only when we are in health of body and mind can we perform our duty to our neighbour'[10]. We need to keep our own sense of distinctiveness in order to be fully connected with our humanity and to be critically aware of what is happening around us, and to take responsibility where it is truly ours. In this way we may perform our duty and maintain our own selfhood. Our selfhood is enhanced when our sense of moral identity is informed by the human responses of sympathy and respect for others.

NOT AFRAID OF FAILING

It is infinitely easier to suffer in obedience to a human command than to accept suffering as free, responsible men. It is infinitely easier to suffer with others than to suffer alone. It is infinitely easier to suffer as public heroes than to suffer apart and in ignominy. It is infinitely easier to suffer physical death, than to endure spiritual suffering. Christ suffered as a free man, alone, apart and in ignominy, in body and in spirit, and since then Christians have suffered with him.[11]

Bonhoeffer draws us to the reality that the crucified Christ was apparently a failure. He had not fulfilled people's expectations that he would be the one to redeem Israel. With hindsight the resurrection changes that view but at the time of his death, failure must have been the operative word after so much self-giving.

His apparent failure was exactly that – it was apparent rather than real. For us there are times when our failure is all too real, when we are conscious, particularly in our relationships with others, of how we have failed and of how we have caused pain. Acceptance of failure is an important part of the way we use suffering rather than prolong it.

It was just another Sunday and just another sermon when suddenly a few words from the preacher caught her attention. He was talking about her, though he did not know it. He said that there are times when we are 'crucified between guilt for the past and fear for the future'.

This is often one point of crucifixion for us as we face failure in our personal life. One half-life may be exchanged for another as we carry guilt and are fearful of what the future holds. Acceptance of failure, however, is acceptance of reality. However painful, reality is the only starting point for real growth and healing. The awareness that we are causing pain to others, or that others are causing us excessive pain leaves us to choose whether we can stay in that situation or not. To stay means to seek to alleviate the pain by working harder at making the situation or the relationships within it work. At other times it is right to free ourselves of the situation. Sometimes 'selfhood begins with a walking away, and love is proved in the letting go.'[12]

Letting go of a situation may enable us to continue to play the song of love but in a different key. In doing this we are exercising a life-giving freedom. We are assuming 'total responsibility for ourselves' and in so doing, 'possess the capacity to reject responsibility that is not truly ours.'[13] Other people involved have their own responsibility and freedom to engage with the situation and grow through it.

The fact that Christ himself has hung at the place of failure reassures us too.[14] For him and for us the place of failure may be the place of reality and therefore of transformation. It is a reminder that living life to the full embraces the possibility and the experience of failure believing that we can grow through it and be strengthened.

In facing our failure and the pain we have inflicted we may seek forgiveness and move on. Facing reality honestly, though excruciating, is also freeing. Pretence is futile.

> There is too much cover up: in both individual and public life people tend to hide failure . . . We need prophets who can confront failure, prophets who, identified with our bankrupt emptiness and experiencing it in themselves, can yet take this very experience into their deepest hearts and find there the heart of God. We need men and women of prayer who can find in defeat and failure the place for knowing God and being open to him, and so can themselves become open gateways between God and our world . . . Such people lovingly assent to the truth which our society conspires to cover up; they face it with us, deeply committed to suffering and failing mankind.[15]

We need these people not as role models but as people who can accompany us as we go through the fires of failure, who understand because they have faced their own sense of oblivion and renewal. They may make forgiveness real for us.

HOPE

Hope will flow from a realistic acceptance of failure, from the acceptance of forgiveness and lessening our fear of the future. In all of this companionship, professional or informal, may be essential. But the hope needs to be real hope.

Hope lies in the centre of our being where God is. It is not a superficial attitude to help us deny the tragedy of our condition. It is built on love and trust rather than denial.

So hope is about living in the present moment with the God who invites us to live his future in the present, to live the Kingdom before the Kingdom is fulfilled. We need not be imprisoned by reality; we can be liberated by it and find hope in God even in darkness. In other words living with hope is not an illusion but

living differently in the present. Perhaps the greatest exponent of
the theology of hope is the German scholar Jurgen Moltmann. He
writes of his time in a concentration camp:

> ... hope came to life as a prisoner accepted his imprisonment,
> affirmed the barbed wire, and in this situation discovered the
> real human being in himself and others. It was not at his release
> but even while in prison that the "resurrection of the dead"
> happened for him.[16]

This hope, based on the acceptance of reality and on trust in God,
is much closer to the New Testament idea of hope than false and
lazy optimism. It implies that hope is a way of living and of loving,
a way of reaching out to others. It's about trust. The secular Greek
word for hope implies 'a rosy look into a sad tomorrow'.[17] In it
pessimism and optimism mingle. But the New Testament use of the
word is based on the Hebrew word for trust. 'The implication is
quiet and secure confidence, and not desperate optimism.'[18]

Real hope does not seek to avoid pain that must legitimately be
borne. It does not harbour fear about being honest with those we
are hurting, or shrink from asking forgiveness. It is above all a hope
based on dedication to the truth.

In chapter 1 I quoted my wife's poem about going down a slide.
It's a poem about the hope that one can still reach beyond oneself,
even in dying.

Two days before she died Jackie gave me a list of people she
wanted to see and slowly in the course of the next day they came,
bringing and finding blessing in their love. That evening the children
played on her bed and she said her goodbyes tenderly and with
dignity. The next morning she asked for everything to be done as
usual. Everything in order, she died soon after noon. The reality
was that she could not survive the disease she had suffered for
many years but she could fulfil a real hope that as she went down
the slide to eternity she could 'lift her face to feel the sun's caress'
and 'scatter the fresh spring flowers from my lap to those who
would stop and watch and enjoy the fun.'[19]

Her words, written in the full knowledge of her disease, remind
us that hope depends on trust in God and not in any specific
outcome. They challenge us to accept our frailty and weakness but
not be overcome by it:

> ... yet those who can face the truth of their condition become
> signs of hope for others. It is not the least of their achievements

that they are broken, incomplete... with their raw edges
reaching always towards the heavens.[20]

ENDINGS AND BEGINNINGS

So often accepting failure and living in hope and trust involves the
acceptance that something has ended – either a relationship, or
the way of living out that relationship. or one's own view of things.
Endings imply grief and being prepared to let our internal map by
which we had been living our lives change and develop. Change is
never easy but the image that Bonhoeffer paints of Jesus dying
alone and in ignominy reminds us that endings are the prelude to
beginnings.

CAUSING SUFFERING TO OTHERS

In this chapter we have looked at the suffering we inflict on others
and at the need to take responsibility by owning our own selfhood.
We recognise that life is painful and that our choices are constrained
sometimes by levels of pain and who bears that pain. We have
seen the dangers of seeking to protect others while recognising
the necessity of protecting them from pain when it can be done
legitimately. We have affirmed the deep hope that is based on love,
truth and trust... and the need sometimes to allow endings to
happen so that new beginnings may take place.

SHARING THE SUFFERING OF OTHERS

Grief cannot be shared for it is mine alone.
Grief is a dying within me,
a great emptiness,
a frightening void.
It is loneliness,
a sickening sorrow at night,
on awakening a terrible dread.
Another's words do not help.
A reasoned argument explains little
for having tried too much.
Silence is the best response to another's grief.
Not the silence that is a pause in speech,
awkward and unwanted,
but one that unites heart to heart.
Love, speaking in silence is the way into
the void of another's grief.
The best of all love comes silently,
and slowly too, to soften the pain of grief,
and begin to dispel the sadness.
It is the love of God, warm and true,
which will touch the grieving heart and heal it.

He looks at the grieving person and has pity,
for grief is a great pain.
He came among us to learn about grief,
and much else too, this Man of Sorrows.
He knows. He understands.
Grief will yield to peace – in time.[1]

Cardinal Basil Hume brings together many of the themes of this chapter in which we explore compassion, listening, humour and the need to care for yourself if you are to care fully for others and be with those who suffer.

BEING ALONGSIDE

Brian Keenan observes that having to live beside a man who is very ill and watch his illness and his helplessness is almost as bad for those who watch as for those who suffer.[2] Being alongside those who are undergoing affliction soon challenges the depth of our relationship. Often someone will shy away from a friend who is going through a personal hell. The one who remains will risk everything as they seek to share suffering which may seem, may indeed be, senseless. There is no way such suffering can be used in a direct way, though indirectly it will shape the lives of those who stand by and may be used by them in real compassionate action later in life when the immediate task of being alongside is over.

Wilfrid Owen and Philip Caputo, a soldier in the Vietnam war, speak out against the senselessness of war. It is said of Wilfrid Owen by a friend that:

> The bond which drew us together was an intense pity for suffering humanity – a need to alleviate it, wherever possible, and an inability to shirk the sharing of it, even when this seemed useless. This was the keynote of Wilfrid's character; indeed it was, simply, Wilfrid. His sensitiveness, his sympathy were so acute, so profound, that direct personal experience and individual development can hardly be said to have existed for him. He could only suffer, or rejoice, vicariously . . . He was naturally silent, but with a silence more expressive than words. He had a wonderful tenderness.[3]

We shall return to this 'communicative silence' later in the chapter. Caputo speaks of another, terrifying silence of one who has been severely wounded.

> I slid down the embankment and splashed over to where the corpsman, Doc Kaiser, was working to save Corporal Rodella. There were gauze and compresses all over his chest and abdomen. One dressing, covering the hole the shrapnel had torn in one of his lungs, was soaked in blood. With each breath he took, pink bubbles of blood formed and burst around the hole. He made a wheezing sound. I tried talking to him, but he could not say anything because his windpipe would fill with

blood. Rodella, who had been twice wounded before, was now in danger of drowning in his own blood. It was his eyes that troubled me most. They were the hurt, dumb eyes of a child who has been severely beaten and does not know why. It was his eyes and his silence and the foaming blood and the gurgling, wheezing sound in his chest that aroused in me a sorrow so deep and a rage so strong that I could not distinguish the one from the other. . . His comrades were around him but he was alone. We could see the look of separation in his eyes. He was alone in the world of the badly wounded, isolated by a pain none could share with him and by the terror of the darkness that was threatening to envelop him.[4]

Sorrow and rage can be either immensely destructive or turned to creative and liberating action in the cause of freedom and truth. These are the real reactions to intense suffering – suffering that makes you rage against the injustice, the feeble explanations of the well-meaning, and the seeming hopelessness and meaninglessness of it all.

Anger which is nursed becomes merely a destructive bitterness. Transformed into deep compassion it can be the driving force for healing and reconciliation. Indeed the element of anger can save real compassion from becoming a sentimental and demeaning pity.[5]

COMPASSION AND PITY

These two words are often used interchangeably but each has a different quality of feeling.

Compassion means 'to suffer with'. It involves going deeply into the experience of another, to recognise that deep bond of humanity which goes beyond surface differences. Compassion shares profoundly the complexity, the beauty, the mystery, the frailty, the vulnerability and the anguish of being human. Compassion does not *look down* at another but *looks across* in an attitude of caring even if that caring reveals itself in sorrow and anger.

Compassion is caring, though we may find such caring only emphasises our own weakness. When such caring is shown then from two weaknesses somehow by the grace of God, strength is born. The Archbishop of Canterbury, preaching in Canterbury Cathedral at the beginning of the 1988 Lambeth Conference drew on the writings of Leonardo da Vinci to express this paradox –

'An arch,' wrote Leonardo da Vinci, 'is nothing else than a strength caused by two weaknesses; for the arch in buildings is made up of two segments of a circle, and each of these segments, being in itself very weak, desires to fall and as one withstands the downfall of the other, the two weaknesses are converted into a single strength.'[6]

If compassion involves an attitude of solidarity, pity can sometimes increase the isolation of those who are suffering. Phyllis Calvert writes:

Sympathy involves sharing something. It is having someone who is somehow able to get close enough to you to share your grief, to share something of the awareness of the situation. It is a very different thing from the experience of pity, which only puts you at a greater distance from the person who is pitying you.[7]

This 'greater distance' is described well by Martin Israel:

. . . pity, a most unbecoming and even dangerous emotion. On the surface it is merely a feeling of tenderness to someone who is in distress, but deeper down there is also an attitude of regret, of feeling sorry, for the person as well. One feels distinctly superior and slightly judgemental as well. One feels that one ought to do something to help, but from the position of being able to distribute one's largesse to someone inferior to oneself. This type of 'duty' is unconsciously demeaning to the afflicted individual.[8]

The distinction between compassion and pity is clear in the relationship between the person who is suffering and the one who is alongside. If material help is needed and given and the approach is one of pity, a dependent relationship may be formed. Compassion respects independence. Compassion keeps a balance between connection and distance and recognises the valuable humanity of both the other and of oneself. Pity may assume it knows best, whereas compassion gives to the person suffering the respect that is needed if they are to respond with freedom to their situation. Pity can so often feel cloying whereas compassion seeks freedom. Pity assumes, compassion listens.

In the professional carer and in the practical care of friends and family compassion reveals itself not only in attitude and emotional awareness but also in competence as far as practical care is concerned.

LISTENING

The woman was obviously disabled. People did not know always how to respond. Sometimes they tried humour, at other times encouragement, sometimes including her in, sometimes carefully not inviting her. There was a great deal of sensitivity but also a great deal of confusion. Above all, she realised, her disability was blinding some people to the fact that she had other needs, other hopes and aspirations for relationships and intimacy. Here too she faced a truth that was not easily shared – she was gay.

Compassion does not assume. Compassion listens to the other and responds to the needs that they understand they have, not to imagined or illusory needs. Compassion is about reality and truth. It necessitates listening and listening well. Those who listen best are those who have listened well to themselves and know their own light and darkness, joy and sorrow, strengths and weaknesses. They have discovered that each of these qualities has the potential to be transformed into its opposite. There is in such listening a deep regard for and a focusing on the needs of the person who is facing suffering.

Such listening is in sharp contrast to some elements of 'healing' ministries which assume that healing is a matter of the strong ministering to the weak and insist that with the 'right' attitude a cure is possible. Such ministries are driven not by the needs of those they seek to serve but by the needs of those who claim to be healers.

When we received Jackie's prognosis we were struck dumb. We knew that she was ill but did not realise that the prognosis would be so short. Fortunately, we had already arranged a holiday and we were glad of the time and space to come to terms with what the consultant had said and to think about plans for the future.

At the hotel we met a Christian couple who seemed to show a genuine warmth and understanding. A few days later we were finding the couple difficult. They claimed to have a healing ministry and insisted that they should exercise it. They waited until I was busy and my wife was alone before offering her the laying on of hands. As she said later, she could not walk away – her legs were already very weak. But she felt used and became very dubious about the healing ministry as a whole.

Those who listen in the name of Christ have a particular responsibility to listen well and to show the respect and sensitivity of true holiness – a genuine holiness that comes from lived discipleship, self knowledge and prayer:

> In the holy we rarely encounter judgement or moralising. Instead, we feel ourselves to be in the presence of an absolute compassion that accepts us as we are. The paradox is that this level of acceptance and sympathy is so overwhelming that it shows us, more clearly than any moraliser could, our own distance from sanctity and our own longing to be given utterly to some great and good thing. An ounce of sanctity does more good for humanity than a ton of morality.[9]

Such listening is not the preserve of orthodox religious people. It is the task of all who accompany others in any way. In both listening and responding the attitude underlying all the words and actions is fundamental. If the attitude is loving, that is deeply committed to the value, choices and growth of the other, then listening becomes healing in itself.

SAFE SPACE

All those being alongside someone who is suffering need to listen. To be realistic, life circumstances will mean that some listen better than others and even a good listener has bad days and vice versa.

> Who will listen?
> Doctor? Social worker? Priest?
> Too busy.

> Crowded surgery,
> Caseload,
> Diary.
> fill the thoughts and minds of these.

> Who will listen?

> Friends abounding,
> already heavy laden
> shrug and go.

Curiosity leads some to question, compare, analyse, solve,
but fail to listen, hear, understand.

Who will listen?

The simple soul,
unfettered by the busyness
sits down and opens coat or bag and heart,
and waits in silence for the other part
to speak, explain, unload, reveal.

And, knowing all, the soul is closed.
No gossip here for future hours.
The load is carried off for prayer
in order that our God may hear
and listening with his greater heart
forgives and comforts,
takes his part,
in Silence.

The poem points to the need for a 'safe space' where one can be
heard in confidence without fear or shame or pretence. The person
listening may also be able to offer expert information, help, or an
opinion.

We may identify four aspects of what it means to be a good
listener:[10]

* Being true to the other person. Sometimes the word 'empathy' is
  used but may have a number of connotations that are not helpful.
  A helpful insight is provided by Richard McMullen:

  My empathetic friend sees the unique mystery that is me.
  Never fully understanding it or deeply exploring it, he allows
  it to be. He sees this mystery and knows it to be the evolving
  me . . . He sees the possibilities for growth and allows it to
  happen . . . He sees the strengths and weaknesses, the potential and limitations, the clear views and the blockages, the
  caring and the selfishness, the harmony and the discord,
  the saint and the sinner. He sees it all and accepts. He sees the
  struggle and the ease of my move towards change . . .[11] (my
  italics)

  'Never fully understanding it' reminds us not to assume that we
  can stand in someone else's shoes. Empathy is a willingness to
  see the world through their perception. It is also the ability

to receive their communication with all our senses so that we understand more than the words alone convey. So we become fully engaged with their world, whilst recognising our distinctiveness in order to respect their individuality and our own – to make it possible to be fully there for them *because* we are distinct and not allowing ourselves to be overwhelmed by their pain. (though, of course, at times we are deeply affected by it).

> Can I be strong enough as a person to be separate from the other? Can I be a sturdy respecter of my own feelings, my own needs, as well as his? . . . Am I strong enough in my own separateness that I will not be downcast by his depression, frightened by his fear, nor engulfed by his dependency? . . . When I can freely feel this strength of being a separate person, then I find that I can let myself go much more deeply in understanding and accepting him because I am not fearful of losing myself.[12]

- Being true to myself for the sake of the other person. Carl Rogers uses the term congruence' to identify that attitude in the listener in which they are able to be aware of their own thoughts and feelings and able to 'be' those thoughts and feelings without wearing a 'mask'. In other words the listener is transparent, fully themselves, and when appropriate for the good of the other, able to communicate those feelings to the other person.[13]
- A generous heart – what Carl Rogers calls 'unconditional positive regard', an outgoing positive attitude without reservations or evaluations – a full and generous acceptance of the other.
- Competence and confidentiality. A friend who is a good listener will naturally let the relationship become *un*equal for the time of listening. One is there for the other. One is laying aside their own agenda, their own concerns, in order to listen fully to the other. In a 'professional' listener there is also a necessary competence and knowledge both intellectual and experiential, which is brought to the listening even if it is never articulated.

SILENCE

In the poem which opens this chapter, Cardinal Basil Hume writes:

> Silence is the best response to another's grief.
> Not the silence that is a pause in speech,
> awkward and unwanted,
> but one that unites heart to heart.

Cardinal Hume speaks of a healing silence which is far removed from the silence which shuns another, which leads to fears and fantasies and which destroys rather than builds relationship. There are times when such silence, even God's silence, is as painful as death for it seems to hide rather than reveal truth. In his powerful novel *Silence* Shusaku Endo relates the story of Christian missionary priests in seventeenth-century Japan. Forced to apostasize one of the priests cannot understand the silence of God. God gives him the answer 'I was not silent. I suffered beside you'.[15] This lies at the heart of much Christian theodicy but when one is enduring the silence of God, this empty silence, then theology seems empty too. A compassionate person alongside us is our strongest ally.

What can such a friend do except listen and then respond honestly and openly? Sometimes that response will be silence; not the empty silence of embarrassment but the deep silence of empathy, a silence that Martin Israel calls 'communicative silence'.[16]

What is so deep and powerfully healing about this silence, is that it reveals something of the true silence of God who can identify with our suffering and who knows his own silence as he faces the darkness of crucifixion.

IMPOTENCE

Sometimes part of our silence in response to suffering is the arresting silence of impotence, of an inability to do or say anything. The acceptance of this impotence is an important part of staying alongside someone rather than walking away. Sheila Cassidy writes of giving a patient the news that his leukaemia had returned:

> The tears ran down his cheeks as he paced my office like a wild animal, hugging to his chest the large teddy bear that lives here. As I watched him weep and listened to him sobbing that he could not face more needles, more sickness, more drug treatment, my heart ached. There were no clever words of reassurance or comfort. All I could do was hug him and then stand there impotently, sharing, in some small measure, his awful pain.[17]

In fact, by being there and sharing some of the pain, Sheila was doing all that could be done at that time. Later, maybe, her skills as a doctor and her personal compassion would not help provide a cure, but might help towards a good death.

This response of presence rather than absence[18] is the essence of healing companionship. All kinds of people may fulfil this role.

When Jackie's disease was progressing rapidly, the doctor suggested that a Macmillan nurse visit us. Jackie felt like saying 'no'. It would be another professional to cope with, somebody else invading the privacy of her home and her pain. Something, however, made her say 'yes'.

It was clear as soon as she arrived that Jan was a special person and nurse. She took time to let Jackie talk, but she also gave time to the children and me. She didn't have a gloomy air, and didn't keep distant from the pain. She offered practical help in small ways, managing to deal with bed sores and cramps and with the intimate details of a young woman who was dying. It soon became a joke that when she came she and I would exchange recipes for soup – Jackie could no longer swallow easily and nutritious home-made soup was a godsend. When Jackie died it was significant that as I walked into church I saw the GP and Jan sitting together.

ANGER

It is well-documented that those who are told they have a terminal illness and those who are bereaved may experience anger as part of their emotional reaction to what life is dealing out to them.[19]

Those who are alongside may well be the object of such anger. God or life in general may be raged against too. Anger may turn in on the sufferer in the form of guilt that a certain life-style precipitated the disease, for example. Such guilt may be based on reality or may be inappropriate.

> The anger encountered ... must not be deplored as selfish or seen as destructive of human value. Very often anger is the struggle of the spirit to survive when a person feels defenceless and betrayed. Anger is at its greatest when it is a cry for love, and the person who suffers silently, stoically, has usually settled for hopelessness. ... liberation comes when anger leads to better self-understanding and better communication.[20]

The person alongside may also have feelings of anger and sorrow. If that part of their suffering is to be used such anger needs to be addressed – not necessarily expressed at the time, but recognised and its source explored. As was said in the introduction, 'an irate person may really have faith, rather than despair'. Anger may change our perception, lifting us out of the rut of hopelessness.

HONESTY

The word 'carer' has been avoided for though it is useful it fails to recognise that the person suffering may actually be doing some care work too. Indeed doing too much caring for others may lead the person suffering to try to protect their 'carer'. To be able to care for another and to be able to listen well requires openness and honesty.

We need to be honest with the person who is suffering and this in itself can be challenging and life-changing – it needs a loving truthfulness rather than a brutal insistence on giving all the facts. Without this kind of care someone who is terminally ill is at the mercy not only of the disease but of a conspiracy of silence or pretence that will eventually become obvious and may betray trust just when trust is most needed.

Clearly some ways are better than others to discover painful truth[21].

> During my consultations, I sat on beds, held hands and talked for hours. There was, I learned, not a single dying human being who did not yearn for love, touch, or communication. Dying patients did not want a safe distance from their doctors. They craved honesty... By listening I came to know that all dying patients know they are dying. It's not a question of 'Do we tell him?' or 'Does he know?'
> The only question to ask is: 'Can I hear him?'[22]

For all those involved there may also be the honesty within oneself as one listens and lives with another. Such self-honesty may be challenged and changed by the circumstances of the suffering.

Everyone thought she was a saint. She had cared for her husband through his illness in an apparently exemplary way – always there for him, organised and efficient in meeting his needs. And she did love him. But their marriage had been very difficult and she had tried to be loyal and had told no-one of her difficulties. If she was honest with herself now that he had died she felt a mixture of emotions but a very powerful one was relief – relief for him that his suffering was over and relief for herself not only because she was relieved from the sheer hard work of caring but because she no longer had to pretend that all was well with the marriage and she could begin to discover a new life.

The woman in question was fortunate that the person in whom she later confided all of this was able to affirm her and not judge her. It would have been so easy for her to have become lost in pointless guilt and remorse.

TOUCH

He'd been visiting her for almost four years. Each time he left he wondered what it was that made her so grateful. After all, she was very deaf and communication was difficult. Often she misheard. At other times there would be long silences.

But on this particular day it became clear. Without thinking as he sat beside her he would often hold her hand, and, as he left, would put one arm round her shoulder as he kissed her cheek.

'Do you know,' she said. 'I really love hands. You can tell so much about a person from their hands. My father had lovely hands. It was so reassuring to take hold of them, and when we prayed as a family and I was very little I would stand at his knee and he would put his arm around my shoulder. I can still feel it. It feels like a touch of God. When you come you bring God near.

The power of touch cannot be overemphasised. It's a power expressed as much when we do not touch as when we do, and careful discernment is needed as to what is appropriate but to fail to touch for fear of misunderstanding is to fail to risk humanity.[23]

HUMOUR

Humour too has its place. It's so easy to imagine that somehow those who suffer prefer hushed tones and steady voices. They may be glad of the necessary rest but, for some, humour is the only way to regain a different perspective on a situation, to transcend the obvious limitations and move beyond them. Brian Keenan and John McCarthy make this point very clearly:

> In that laughter we discovered something of what life really is. We were convinced by the conditions we were kept in and the lives that we managed to lead that if there was a God that God was, above all else, a comedian. In humour, sometimes

hysterical, sometimes calculated, often childish, life was returned to us.

However, on each occasion that we found ourselves rising above the grinding monotony, something happened to warn us that reality is not always comic.[24]

Our humour was not heroism, quite the reverse. It was a way of putting the previous night at a distance from us, screened behind humour and affection, so we could take control of it before it took control of us.[25]

An attempt at humour at the wrong time may not only be insensitive but may betray a lack of understanding of the needs of the other. Sensitivity is balanced by risk and humour is often invaluable.[26] As Keenan discovered, there is humour in God. Certainly at times of crisis and trauma, as well as at times of great joy, that has often been my experience:

It comes from the depth of my being,
    this 'Yes' to God.
It tears me to pieces and makes me whole.
It yearns in my deepest desire,
and gives birth to the deepest
fresh born,
      frisson,
        fun –
God's joy.
It finds a deep, pot bellied
      laughing echo –
a God who understands

And listening to
      the silence of my
    'Yes'
the sound of God's joy overwhelms
    though the whisper on
      God's breath is so gentle.
        Yes, he says, Yes.[27]

CARING FOR YOURSELF

Perhaps the hardest lesson for those who long to care for others is that it simply cannot be done without caring for oneself.

It's very tempting to want to be there, to be 'on call' if not 'on duty'. For the carer in the home situation this may be the case rather than a matter of choice. But there are limits to the love we can offer. We need something else – beauty, recreation, rest and refreshment – to look after ourselves.

Whenever circumstances permit it is important to create and respect boundaries in order to maintain one's own sense of well-being. If we give we also need to receive. Some of that receiving will happen in the giving but some will also need to come from elsewhere. We serve those for whom we care best by making space for the 'elsewhere'.[28]

Caring for others over a period of time involves not only day-to-day giving, but a deeper giving of the fibre of our being. In a memorable phrase Sheila Cassidy writes, 'Therapists aren't born. . . they are forged like steel in a furnace'.[29] It's true of many who accompany others on a professional basis, as well as of those who look after friends or family for years. For the professional, the necessary training involves working on oneself and on the raw material of one's own life. There is then an awareness of and the use of one's own vulnerability.

LEARNING FROM SUFFERING

Kahlil Gibran writes, 'Your pain is the breaking of the shell that encloses your self-understanding'[30]. It's a line that can be difficult to take but does portray a truth – that suffering can be our teacher. We can learn from our own suffering, from our reflection on the suffering of others and directly from those who suffer. In his novel *Scar Tissue* Michael Ignatieff's character Moe is a great teacher:

> I tell him (Moe) that I will not pray to someone who makes him suffer like this. His mischievous eyes do not lose their sense of humour. Letter by letter, more words emerge on the big screen:
> 'I lie here; I cannot move; however I can listen, think, pray. How is it I feel love? and where is it coming from?'[31]

Moe has a good sense of humour, and beside his bed there are pictures of his family, an icon, and a poster; 'Nuclear Free Zone: No Enemas Here'![32]

BEING ALONGSIDE THOSE WHO SUFFER

In this chapter as we have explored the task of being alongside, we have recognised the cost and the joy of true compassion. Suffering can be our teacher by which we learn how to love. That does not excuse the suffering. There can be no excuse for unnecessary suffering. But it does remind us that suffering need not be empty and that it has the potential of great riches. We have recognised too the importance of humour.

8

SHARING THE SUFFERING OF GOD

A memory of Kreisler once:
At some recital in this same city,
The seats all taken, I found myself pushed
On to the stage with a few others,
So near that I could see the toil
Of his face muscles, a pulse like a moth
Fluttering under the fine skin
And the indelible veins on his smooth brow.

I could see, too, the twitching of the fingers,
caught temporarily in art's neurosis,
As we sat there or warmly applauded
This player who so beautifully suffered
For each of us upon his instrument.

So it must have been on Calvary
In the fiercer light of the thorns' halo:
The men standing by and that one figure,
The hands bleeding, the mind bruised but calm,
Making such music as lives still.
And no one daring to interrupt
Because it was himself that he played
And closer than all of them the God listened.[1]

R.S.Thomas sums up what it means to suffer with God – to be who we are, in our particular situation and suffering as a result. . . 'it was himself that he played.' In this chapter we explore what that means for Jeremiah, Jesus, and ourselves. Any theology of suffering comes not from a study of theology alone but from reflection on a life lived for and in God. Richard Wurmbrand, a pastor who spent three years in solitary confinement in a cell thirty feet below the ground, writes:

I once tried to explain 'systematic theology' to a Russian pastor of the Underground church, who had never seen a whole New Testament. Systematically, I began to explain to him the teaching about the Godhead, about its unity in three persons, the teaching about original sin, about the fall, about salvation, about the Church, about the sacraments, about the Bible as infallible revelation. He listened attentively. When I had finished, he put to me a most surprising question: 'Have those who thought out these theological systems and wrote them down in such perfect order ever carried a cross?' He went on: 'A man cannot think systematically even when he has a bad toothache. How can a man who is carrying a cross think systematically? But a Christian has to be more than the bearer of a heavy cross; he shares Christ's crucifixion. The pains of Christ are his, and the pains of all creation. . . . can there be that kind of thought on a cross? Jesus himself thought unsystematically on the cross. He began with forgiveness; he dreamed of a paradise in which a robber had a place; then he despaired that perhaps there might be no place in paradise even for him, the Son of God. He felt himself forsaken. . . . Then he surrendered his spirit into the Father's hands. But there followed no serenity, only a loud cry. Thank you for what you have been trying to teach me. I have the impression that you were only repeating, without much conviction, what others have taught you. Systematic theology of any kind is impossible in Christianity.'[2]

Donald Nicholl argues that there is no exclusive *locus* for theology but that, following the example of St Paul our *locus* should be one where we are constantly ready for dislocation ' . . . because it is only by being dislocated that one is enabled to see and to witness to the truths of our faith'.[3] Jeremiah and Jesus knew all about being in such a place where the enormous love of God and the reality of the world including its suffering is not avoided, denied, or toned down. Before looking at these two men of dislocation we need first therefore to explore the holding together of apparent contradictions, especially suffering and love.

TRUST-WITHOUT-STRINGS

Simone Weil writes:

God created through love and for love. God did not create

anything but love itself, and the means to love. He created love in all its forms. He created beings capable of love from all possible distances. Because nobody other could do it, he himself went to the greatest possible distance, the infinite distance. This infinite distance between God and God, this supreme tearing apart, this agony beyond all others, this marvel of love, is the crucifixion. Nothing can be further from God than that which has been made accursed.

This tearing apart over which supreme love places the bond of supreme union, echoes perpetually across the universe in the midst of the silence, like two notes, separate and yet melting into one, like pure and heart rending harmony. This is the Word of God. The whole of creation is nothing but its vibration. . . . those who persevere in love hear this note from the very lowest depths into which affliction has thrust them. From that moment they can no longer have any doubt.[4]

This ability to let two notes sound together until they find a harmony is the means of encounter by which situations may find transformation and hope. For example, we know that the strongest relationships are those where both partners are able to sustain and express their unique personhood. Love embraces rather than levels out difference – though some accommodation to each other makes for a more peaceful life.

Indeed the holding together of differences allows the possibility of each throwing light on the other, providing fresh revelations. It also provides the 'human grace' by which one enables the other to become more truly themselves. In any theology of suffering this way of paradox is often the only way.[5]

We have to hold together the apparent randomness of life and a belief that God's ultimate purpose is good, the beauty of creation with its brutality, the possibility of the enormous love of God and the darkness that at times pervades the world, society and our own being.

How might we hold these together unless we are prepared to be at the place of dislocation, unless we are prepared for the crucifixion and resurrection to be a paradigm for how life is? And how might we be willing to be at that place unless we have a 'trust-without-strings' in God? 'Trust-without-strings' does not shrugs its shoulders at the apparent capriciousness of God. 'Trust-without-strings' is the kind of trust that Simone Weil describes in the quotation above: 'those who persevere in love hear this note from the very lowest

depths into which affliction has thrust them. From that moment
they can no longer have any doubt.'

Although at a deep level there may be lack of doubt, there is no
lack of struggle. Quite the opposite. One who knows trust-without-
strings will know crucifixion and *ultimate* struggle – the tension
between the presence and the apparent absence of God, between
knowing the love of God and feeling the full force of evil, between
the temptation to live the false self which pleases others or being the
real self that seems often to challenge others.

It is trust in God without claiming anything for oneself or
demanding any outcome apart from knowing, desiring and risking
that God's will is done. It is the trust of dislocation, of brokenness
and vulnerability, a trust which says, 'Yes' to God even when there
is no obvious reason to say, 'Yes'. It is a trust which recognises that
death needs to be embraced if life is to be full. It is to know that, 'the
wish to avoid suffering can imprison, can stultify . . .'[6] and that, 'by
excluding death from our life we cannot live a full life, and
by admitting death into our life we enlarge and enrich it.[7]

This trust is not indifferent in the sense of evading or ignoring
suffering. It feels suffering to the core. It is not masochistic,
assuming suffering as its own when it could be alleviated or
avoided. It is ready to suffer and to share the suffering of others if
that is the true approach to what life is bringing.

It means being prepared to change, to let go of learnt ways of
seeing things and habitual responses to situations. It means being
inwardly free to become more truly oneself and more truly one with
God who can take our tragedies and transfigure them into new life,
provided we have grieved with him over the tragedy and suffered
with him the death that change entails.

> Do you think it is easy to change ?
> Ah, it is very hard to change and be different.
> It means passing though the waters of oblivion.[8]

THE ABYSS OF EMPTINESS AND THE ABYSS OF LOVE

'Trust-without-strings' takes us to the heart of the crucifixion and
resurrection, and to the belief that God can transfigure, or transform,
the darkness of the world. 'To live as Easter people requires vision
and grace. It demands of us that we do not try to avoid the world's
pain and darkness but rather bear it and even dare to bear it for
others believing that all darkness, all suffering, all agony and

dereliction can be redeemed. To live this way is to trust absolutely in the Father's love, as Jesus trusted. It is to believe that, in God, nothing is wasted'.[9]

Such trust will sometimes know the fullness of God's presence and often the emptiness that is its corollary. It will work towards its own transformation and the transformation of society but always knowing that the deeper transformation is God's prerogative. It will engage with life and the world but also be wary of false attachments which hold it back from fulfilling its 'Yes' to God. It will know both the abyss of emptiness and the abyss of God's love.

> And from the darkness of my death
>   and his,
> Is life restored
> and love and truth have met
>   and kissed
> and desire runs behind
>   like a toddler through a flowery field.
> And all the agony and sweat
>   and crucifixion nails
> give way to birth and tears
> and I am home again and full of love.

Abyss is a strong word yet it is the only word for that emptiness within which only God can fill but which we so painfully try to fill with all but God until either life experience strips us of everything and the abyss itself cries out for recognition, or in response to God we consent to let him strip us down. For some childhood love will already have entered that abyss and provided some confidence in life and in love. For others the abyss feels like an achingly empty nothingness and a source of trenchant fear, as I know to my cost:

> Fear has been my habitat, my landscape,
> for, oh, so many years.
> And I,
> not wanting to be held by it,
> have battled through its limitations,
> sometimes cowered in its shadows,
> at others, at great costs, battered down its iron walls,
> scrambled through its thickets of uncertainty
> traversed its gorges of paralysis
> in order to move on –
> an assault course just to live.

Fear has never been my friend.
It's locked me in,
isolated me,
denied me, me.

Fear has never been my friend,
I have fought it far too long.
It's time to stop the fighting,
time to learn to live from love,
let fear take its proper place,
to learn to live from God within,
at one with him.

This emptiness can lie at the heart of society and be revealed in times of conflict, fear and chaos. Society encourages us to maintain a distance from the abyss of being alone by using drugs and alcohol, shopping 'therapy' taken to extremes, or by spending hours alone on the internet. These are all ways of trying to meet the demands of our unloved shadow side.

Unless the emptiness is acknowledged in ourselves and in society; unless it is grieved and mourned, change is blocked. The fear of the abyss means that we hang onto the past in an attempt to feel secure rather than risk what is new.

JEREMIAH[10]

Jeremiah, a prophet during the period in which Jerusalem was facing its downfall, could not bear to see his people pretend that all was well when the emptiness of their world was obvious. He berates both the religious and the political leadership:

> Do not trust in these deceptive words, 'This is the Temple of the Lord, the Temple of the Lord, the Temple of the Lord.' (7: 4) They have treated the wound of my people carelessly, saying, 'Peace, peace', when there is no peace. (6: 14 and 8: 11).

Jeremiah's message is very tough. He is to 'pluck up and to pull down, to destroy and to overthrow, to build and to plant'. He is to encourage his people to relinquish the past and be ready to receive the future, to acknowledge emptiness in order that they may find fulfilment. He has to call them to be content to live with loss and grief without certainty of what comes next, trusting that what comes will be for their healing. That healing will be God's doing (30. 17) and will only come about when the wound itself is recognised (30: 12, 13, 15). All Jeremiah has to sustain him is God's word, 'I am with you' – words that can feel like meagre rations when you are caught in the middle of religious, political or personal turmoil. Indeed Jeremiah may well have felt 'doubt, depression and failure of nerve'[11] 'Cursed be the day on which I was born !' (20: 14). In the midst of this Jeremiah is sustained because his ministry and life are rooted in God. He has this trust-without-strings. It is a trust which comes to realise that life is not about being in a state of equilibrium. It is about transformation in God. The God of transformation is not the safe God of conventional religion but the God who has been discovered in the heat of the refiner's furnace.[12] The words of Job speak for Jeremiah too, 'If I go forward he is not there; or backward, I cannot perceive him; on the left he hides and I cannot behold him; I turn to the right but I cannot see him. But he knows the way that I take; when he has tested me I shall come out like gold'.

Quite simply, Jeremiah can dare to stand against the powers of his day because he has been shaped and formed by God. His life experience opens up for him a new vista of God's heart. In his own pain and anguish he recognises the pain and anguish and grief of God who, as Jesus will in his lifetime, weeps over Jerusalem.

The way for Jeremiah is not the safe way. It is the way of trust. For him there is little equilibrium:

> Jeremiah does not wish to be that much at risk. There is a yearning for a season of equilibrium . . . The poems ask for God to let some things be settled on Jeremiah's terms. Jeremiah must struggle in his life of call and conflict. It makes a difference if equilibrium is taken as the norm, as the way life is supposed to be, or if transformative tension is the way life really is. Jeremiah understands and embraces that transformative tension in the life he has been given from God, and he does not regard it as an intrusion in a life that would otherwise be marked by equilibrium . . . the yearning for equilibrium is an idolatrous escape from reality. . . If we do not experience the pain, rage, and dis-ease that goes with such dis-equilibrium we may be missing out on our call.[13]

This is not to argue that we should cause turmoil and trauma or look for suffering, but should it be our lot then accepting its reality with confidence in God is the way that dissolution becomes renewal.

In analysing the possibilities open to those who are aware that they are living in a declining civilisation Dr Philip Toynbee writes:

> ... distinguishes four principles – archaism, futurism, detachment, transfiguration. *Archaism* is the yearning for a past golden age, *futurism* is a phantasy of a new age utterly unrelated to that which already exists, and the quest of it is often pursued by violent means; *detachment* (for which 'escapism' would be a better word . . .) is an escape into contemplation; but *transfiguration* is a faith whereby 'we bring the total situation as we ourselves participate in it, into a larger context which gives it a new meaning.'[14]

This is what Jeremiah is doing. He is prepared to stand at the place of nothing – of non-existence – and assert that it is a real place where the past can be relinquished and the future received. So his word is harsh yet hopeful. It comes from the place of dislocation, of transformative tension and of 'transformed imagination',[15] of seeing death and diminishment in a wider context which gives it different meaning.

Brueggemann writes:

> In God's attentive pain, healing happens. Newness comes. Possibilities are presented. But it all depends on being present with God in the hurt, which is incurable until God's hint of healing is offered.[16]

JESUS

> A lone young shepherd lived in pain
> withdrawn from pleasure and contentment,
> his thoughts fixed on a shepherd-girl
> *his heart an open wound with love.*
>
> He weeps, but not from the wound of love,
> there is no pain in such affliction,
> even though the heart is pierced,
> he weeps in knowing he's been forgotten.
>
> That one thought: his shining
> one has forgotten him, is such great pain
> that he bows to brutal handling in a foreign land,
> *his heart an open wound with love.*

The shepherd says: I pity the one
Who draws himself back from my love,
and does not see the joy of my presence
though my heart is an open wound with love for her.

After a long time he climbed a tree,
and spread his shining arms,
and hung by them, and died,
his heart an open wound with love.[17]

This poem by St John of the Cross identifies powerfully with a transformative tension that holds together both love and the pain of love – his heart an open wound. We find echoes in the writing of Jurgen Moltmann:

As injured love, the wrath of God is not something that is inflicted, but a divine suffering of evil. It is a sorrow which goes through his opened heart. He suffers in his passion for his people.[18]

Sorrow piercing the heart is the beginning and end of Jesus' ministry from the presentation in the Temple to the crucifixion, from Luke 2: 35 to John 19: 34. This sorrow is not isolated sorrow, isolated pain; it is sorrow and pain held in transformative tension with the love, healing and grace of God – 'sorrow and love flow mingling down'.[19]

In Christ we see this transformative tension writ large, a tension held by trust-without-strings which reveals itself in love.

What can we say of Christ? 'He is the image of the invisible God . . . in him all the fullness of God was pleased to dwell' (Colossians 1: 15 and 19), 'we have seen his glory, the glory as of a father's only son, full of grace and truth' (John 1: 14), 'he was in the form of God' (Philippians 2: 6), and yet, he came 'not to be served but to serve and to give his life as a ransom for many' (Mark 10: 45), 'he emptied himself' (Philippians 2: 7), he is a 'stumbling block to Jews and foolishness to Gentiles' (1 Corinthians 1: 23).

No wonder that some recognised him and others could see nothing special in him. He both revealed and concealed the face of God and spoke in parables so that they who could see and hear might understand.

Paul Ricoeur suggests that, 'people are changed not by ethical urging but by transformed imagination'.[20] So it is that Jesus seeks to transform people's imagination so that they might see God in their midst and the possibilities and joys of the Kingdom.

Jesus did this not just by his words but by his very life and death.

Conventional religion left her cold. It did not speak at all to her situation – at least if it did it felt only like condemnation. After all she had been married and had an affair. She was divorced and her life was far from pure. Religion had nothing left to say to her. Then she met a friend who went to church and wasn't at all what she imagined. He didn't judge her, didn't try to change her, but as she showed an interest in God he gently introduced her to the God he knew and left her to think for herself and discover what she believed. He wanted nothing from her, unlike some other men. He offered only friendship but as she came to know him that very friendship challenged her for she saw how his life was at one with what he believed. He wasn't perfect, he did not always obey the 'rules'. He simply loved his God and knew God's love and was able to show it to her.

It is perhaps in the language of symbol and metaphor, poetry and undemanding love that Jesus speaks most clearly to the people of his and our day. But we are challenged not just to admire and love him, but to follow him, to be transformed into what is most true in us and therefore most Christ-like. Here then is another paradox: that undemanding love freely given is held in conjunction with an ultimate challenge to give everything, to consent to transformation through death to life as a way of living.

We need to explore some of these themes further, particularly the cross, our suffering and his, transformed imagination and the possibility of consenting to abandonment.

THE CROSS

The cross is the everyday suffering that comes our way because we are who we are and, for some of us, the suffering we bear because we seek to follow Jesus. It is important to recognise both aspects of our cross in contrast to Jesus' cross. His cross was one he consented to carry and bear. His was a chosen vulnerability[21] and not one thrust upon him by illness, accident, war or disease – 'his face was set towards Jerusalem' (Luke 9: 53).

In death, as in birth, Jesus was entering the abyss, the emptiness of humankind without God and revealing within it the abyss of

God's love. His suffering, death and resurrection is the transforming tension in which redemption and healing happens.

Holy Saturday seems strangely still. Luke carefully tells us so. The women prepare the spices on the Friday but rest on the Saturday. Christ though is working, even in death. The tradition of the harrowing of hell is perhaps the epitome of extravagant love. It's a profound tradition which I have encountered in two ways. Several years ago I was leading a man thorough the Ignatian exercises in which there is a meditation on hell. The man was in tears. In his prayer he had 'seen' Jesus descending to hell and reaching out his hand to those who were lost. Nothing had ever revealed just how much love God offers. The experience changed his whole perception of God.

A couple of years later I went to see an exhibition of Russian icons and one in particular struck me – the Descent into Hell (Anastasis)[22] . In it Jesus stands above the broken gates of hell holding Adam and Eve by the hand. He is leading them from the black pit of hell to freedom and eternal life. The exhibition catalogue says, 'This moment is the culmination of the mission of Christ in the world, the redemption of the first man and woman and therefore of humanity as a whole'.[23]

Here then is another image of extravagant love: Jesus going the ultimate distance to save us. He pours himself out in love. He goes the ultimate distance to be with us in our personal hell, but also to bring us out. He is with us in our suffering yet reaches beyond it. Here is the epitome of divine love.

The fact that Jesus chose to accept suffering means that as one Greek Orthodox nun has put it, 'he blessed suffering and suffering enters into the mystery of the divine.'[24]

In this way the cross gave suffering a new level of meaning and purpose. It did not and does not justify suffering. Too often the strong have exploited the weak by suggesting that suffering should be identified with Christ's passion instead of being radically addressed in the structures and patterns of relationships, in society and in world affairs. The cross offers hope not by avoiding the need to alleviate suffering where we can, but by making it possible that even in suffering we may become more truly who we are, and may come to an experience of the divine. Jurgen Moltmann writes of his experiences in prison camp, 'It is not the experiences which are important but the one who is experienced in them'.[25]

OUR SUFFERING AND HIS

It is important therefore to consider how our suffering relates to Jesus' suffering on the cross. And here we meet a stunning 'transformative tension' for his suffering both identifies with ours and is distinct from it.

His suffering identifies with ours on a number of levels. First because he was completely human; and second, because his suffering was not limited by time or space he continues to suffer in his people. If we invite him, he carries our unique suffering *with* us, not *instead* of us. When we look at the crucified we may see not a reflection of ourselves and our suffering, not just another person who knows what it's like to suffer. We can see our suffering carried by one who identifies with us but is distinct from us, one who holds in tension heaven and earth, and who longs for our healing.

We too can identify with his suffering:

> In Jesus' death black slaves saw themselves, and they unleashed their imagination in describing what they felt and saw ... His death was a symbol of their suffering, trials and tribulations in an unfriendly world. They knew the agony of rejection and the pain of hanging from a tree ... Because black slaves knew the significance of the pain and shame of Jesus' death, they found themselves by his side.[26]

We can celebrate not only the identification but the distinctiveness of Jesus' suffering – for his suffering has the power to transform ours, and the distinction means that he can share our suffering explicitly. There is a paradigm here of every professional therapeutic relationship where the person who has suffered and can contain their suffering is often most able to bear the suffering of another. Jesus gives space to our suffering so that he may respect us *and* share our pain.

This combination of connectedness and distinctiveness is the means by which healing is wrought. By healing we mean the entry of grace into a situation which enables meaning, hope and freedom to be given whatever the physical circumstances.

TRANSFORMED IMAGINATION

This holding together of opposites and seeing God through paradox is very much the understanding of God expressed by Eckhart.

Cyprian Smith describes this understanding when he talks of the 'clash of contraries':

> I am destined for union with God; I was created for that; and will find fulfilment only in that. But I cannot attain this by remaining where I am now; I have to die somehow to the life I am living: so as to find the new life in God. This death and rebirth must involve my *whole* self, not only my daily life, but my thought and speech. No part of me, not even my mind and tongue, can get through to God without passing through the clash of contraries.[27]

Here is a holistic understanding of the need for transformation and healing to embrace the whole of us, and change our understanding. The ability to allow our internal maps by which we order our lives to be altered by new circumstances and new perceptions lies at the heart of healthy encounter with life. We need to transform the way we see things. They are transformed not only by reflection on life experience and in the encounter with others but also by things which help us gain a different perspective – awareness of the wider world, the needs of others, literature, music, drama, art, prayer, ritual, gesture, celebration, humour and even, sometimes, anger.

Often a new perspective can release us from a prison of our own making, a set way of seeing things that no longer fits what life holds for us. When we dare to walk into this new way of thinking we can dare to leave the old life behind and make tentative steps towards a new one. Sometimes we seek such a transformed way of seeing things. At other times we are forced into it by life, and have to face loss and grief, loss of familiarity, known ways of doing things, patterns of thought that have given security and comfort. In other words, the transformation can feel risky and insecure – no wonder the religious authorities hounded both Jeremiah and Jesus.

Transformed imagination can also be a gift. We realise that to see things differently changes a situation entirely and we feel the rush of excitement as we walk through an imaginary wall that had been blocking our progress. It may mean that we have to accept some uncertainty between the death of the old and the birth of the new.

> Do you know what happens inside a chrysalis, a butterfly chrysalis? It's weird. First the caterpillar grows and all that stuff and then it makes a chrysalis for itself, spins it out of its own flesh, and then that hardens. I suppose I'd always thought that

there was a fairly straightforward growing process inside, that the caterpillar grew wings and so on and so forth and then popped out. But it isn't like that at all. There's a total disintegration inside, complete, all the cells break down, break right down into primal slime, into complete yuck. They break down into nothing and then they reform into a butterfly. Isn't that amazing? It seems like a tiny proof of resurrection. That it can happen at all.[28]

Sara Maitland uses the emotive words 'primal slime, complete yuck' to describe the empty feeling that often accompanies periods of great change – periods of nothingness. In the next chapter we shall look at the dynamic of transformation as we explore what it means to share Christ's suffering. And in chapter 11 we shall explore the experience of 'primal slime, complete yuck' in terms of dealing with times of impasse in our life.

9

SUFFERING, LIFE AND PRAYER

Thus naked am I nailed, O man, for thy sake.
I love thee, then love me. Why sleepest thou? Awake!
Remember my tender heart-root for thee brake,
With pains my veins constrained to crack.
    Thus was I defaced,
    Thus was my flesh raced,
    And I to death chased,
Like a lamb led unto sacrifice,
Slain I was in most cruel wise.

Dear brother, none other thing I desire
But give me thy heart free, to reward mine hire.
I am he that made the earth, water and fire . . .

   . . . I have purveyed a place full clear
For mankind, whom I have bought dear.[1]

This anonymous medieval poem echoes that of Swinburne which begins chapter 5 on God's desire that we respond to him freely – 'give me thy heart free'.

Giving ourselves freely to God, abandonment to God, may take us deeper into suffering as we share the dynamic of Christ's life – that paschal mystery which takes him from life, through suffering to death and then through death to resurrection. To share this dynamic requires us to make a total response of our life and prayer.

THE CORKSCREW

To have an image of this dynamic is essential to an understanding of sharing Christ's suffering. We do not share his suffering for the sake of it, but so that this dynamic may go forward, if not immediately for us, then for others and for the world.

Pondering this dynamic as I was preparing to preach one Holy Week led me to talk about an old-fashioned corkscrew with a wooden handle and a sharp spiralling prong. It can be a symbol of the events of Christ's and our life.

In taking up the corkscrew, piercing and digging into the cork, then pulling out the cork and pouring the wine, there is a dynamic. Life – ours and Christ's – is like that too. If we think too much about each step in the process we lose sight of its meaning. The meaning is in the dynamic.

Then there's a spiral, a circular movement going deeper. As suffering pierces us, we often find ourselves addressing situations and issues which seem all too familiar, as though we are going round in circles. In fact we are moving in a corkscrew movement – coming to the same place but at a deeper or higher level.

Then there's a piercing. There is suffering. If we see only our suffering it fills every available space, overwhelming us with its pain and persistence. Only for the sake of the joy that lies ahead, deeper within as well as further away, can we endure the cross. As part of the dynamic the piercing has to be done to release the wine. For Christ the piercing is for our sake. It is the release of the wine of the messianic banquet.

The process has a purpose. Although pain and suffering seem to have a Good Friday intensity and though at times we cannot see beyond the events of Holy week, the whole dynamic assures us that through life or death we shall taste the wine of the Kingdom, we shall share Christ's life, his glory as well as his suffering.

The corkscrew is itself a cross. To enter into this dynamic is only possible through grace, through the knowledge of the love of God that draws us with Christ through our dyings into new life.

SHARING CHRIST'S SUFFERINGS

In this context of *dynamic* and *process* we may explore what it means to share Christ's suffering:

> I am now rejoicing in my sufferings for your sake, and in my flesh I am completing what is lacking in Christ's afflictions for the sake of his body, that is, the church. (Colossians 1:24)

The author of the letter to the Colossians, whether Paul or not, is clearly sharing something of Paul's understanding of the place of suffering in Christian discipleship. What produces rejoicing is not the suffering itself – there is no room for gratuitous suffering in

Christianity – but his relationship with the body of believers and the 'person' of Christ (see, for example, Philippians 3: 8).

Colossians 1 :24 is a verse which has given scholars much food for thought and any suggestion as to its exact meaning is tentative. Nevertheless it seems possible that the 'afflictions' of Christ finds a parallel in Colossians 2: 11 which tells us of the 'circumcision of Christ' not in terms of the physical circumcision of the Christ child but, metaphorically speaking, that of the christian fellowship. 'Christ's afflictions' may relate to the afflictions of his followers and in particular those of Paul. Indeed the Greek word *Koinonia*, or fellowship, is often used of the sufferings of those who will follow Christ and those engaged in the apostolic ministry (Matt 24: 9, John 16: 33, Acts 11: 19, 14: 22, Romans 5: 3, 8: 35, Phil 4: 14) and is not used of Christ's earthly sufferings. Paul is therefore suffering in solidarity with others who are suffering as a result of following Christ. He is 'filling' up his share in the suffering of the Church, in the sufferings of Christ in his body, the 'fellowship' of believers. Like Jeremiah before him, Paul is not only speaking God's word, but living it in his own body – 'it was himself that he played'[2]. But unlike Jeremiah, Paul is not just 'playing himself'; Christ is also 'playing' and suffering in him.

THE FELLOWSHIP OF SUFFERING

Paul expresses the experience of suffering with Christ and for Christ as a privilege (Phil 1: 29), all that he longs for (Phil 3: 10f.), and as the experience of Christ living in him (Gal 2: 20). He also understands it in terms of sharing in the suffering of the fellowship of all who seek to follow Christ.

In order to understand this fellowship of suffering we need to look further at the New Testament understanding of fellowship and sharing in the life of Christ. *Koinonia*[3] is primarily about fellowship in Christ (1 Cor. 1: 9), and so with all other believers (1 John 1: 7 cf. John 15).

This fellowship in salvation (Jude 1: 3) and in the mystery of the gospel (Eph 3: 9, Phil 1: 5) becomes visible in the breaking of bread (1 Cor 10: 16), in the apostles' fellowship (Acts 2: 42) and in caring for those in need (Rom 12: 13, 15: 27, 2 Cor 6: 6, 8: 4.). All of these are outward expressions of the inner fellowship with Christ and with each other. It also involves sharing in the suffering of Christ (Phil 3: 10), in his comfort (2 Cor 1), in his resurrection (Phil 3: 10f.), *and* in his glory (Rom 8: 17f., Ephesians 3: 13, 1 Peter 1: 11,4: 13, 5:1) for the sake of the kingdom (1 Thess 1: 5), the gospel (2 Thess 1: 8) and the fellowship (Col 1: 24). Primarily though it is a participation in the life of Christ and in the paschal mystery of the death and resurrection of Christ. Rather than having a fellowship of suffering we have a fellowship of Christ embracing his suffering *and glory*.

FELLOWSHIP OF SUFFERING AND GLORY

The image of the butterfly is a helpful one. In the light of knowing from experience that a butterfly will emerge it is possible to have hope even in the yuck. It is also possible to trust if we know that in the yuck there are genes which ensure its transformation. Hope and trust are also encouraged if we have a primary understanding of a loving creator.

Nevertheless, the yuck is still yuck and the breakdown is traumatic in practice. So it is when we suffer. Caught in suffering's grasp we may at times experience only the yuck. Sharing Christ's suffering and glory gives another perspective. In the light of the resurrection, the basis of Christian hope (1 Peter 1: 3), we can hope that our suffering will give way, in life or death, to glory. It will not be human glory – the praise of those around us for how stoic we have been or how loving despite our pain. It will be God's glory revealed in those who maintain a loving trust in him through the vicissitude of life. Humanly speaking they may not be stoic. They may be afraid and anxious and crying out but in their honesty they live their truth for God. It is all that he requires.

Similarly it is possible to trust, not because the experience of yuck makes us have any reason for trust, but because we may have experienced that transforming dynamic before or may have witnessed it in others, or have caught the vision of it in Christ.

The yuck gives us no reason to believe in a loving God, unless we have grown to know him as loving at other times or unless we experience even in our suffering some glimpse of that love either through the love of people around us or by some other less tangible means.

In other words, sharing the fellowship of suffering and glory is not necessarily about finding hope, love and trust in the immediate circumstances of our situation. This is the lesson we learnt too from Jeremiah – the need to 'bring the total situation as we ourselves participate in it, into a larger context which gives it new meaning.'[4]

To do this means to consent as Jeremiah did to a life in conflict as a result of his call, or to consent to offering our present circumstances to God as part of this dynamic. This second form of consent needs careful explanation. It is not a fatalistic attitude of resigning oneself to the situation as it is. It is rather a surrendering of oneself to God in that situation, desiring to work with him in its transformation. The former is 'signing off'. The latter is 'signing on' – offering God space in our lives in which to transfigure all that we are and experience.

ASPECTS OF SHARING IN CHRIST'S SUFFERING NOW

We might name four aspects of sharing in the suffering of Christ, recognising that he shares in our humanity (Hebrew 2: 4) and in our personal suffering:

- sharing deeply in the life of God
- sharing his suffering and grief in response to the needs of his people and the world
- sharing his suffering in seeking to relieve the needs of others
- sharing his suffering by offering the suffering of our humanity to him and bearing whatever comes our way as a result of discipleship

All these sufferings involve our whole life and prayer and as they are held in Christ need to be seen with a paschal overview for, as the Carthusians say, 'Love has a paschal rhythm'.

SHARING DEEPLY IN THE LIFE OF GOD

Sharing deeply in the life of God means sharing in this dynamic of God – having his spirit (Gk. *dunamis*) breathe and live in us so that whatever our lives hold for us, they also hold God's transforming gene.

In sharing this dynamic, in allowing God's spirit to work in us, we may fulfil our humanity and be drawn to union with God.

> Christ showed us how to really become human beings ... We cannot say that we had any right to the divine work of reunification (cf. Eph. 1: 10) that was accomplished through Christ... God does not undermine our humanity, he protects and insures it ... When God draws the creature to himself, the creature becomes all the more important. When God draws

near, he makes the glow of our humanity shine even more
brightly before us. He heightens our true greatness as human
beings.[5]

Johannes Metz conveys the importance of this prime motivation
of God – to become one with us and to reconcile us to himself. The
aim is not self-realisation or perfection but union with God. If this
is the aim then knowing our own poverty means that we know *only*
God can do this work of reconciliation and of transformation.

This view of God's activity or God's initiative can change our
way of seeing things. The question is no longer, 'What can I do for
God?', or even, 'What does God want me to do for him?', but, 'What
is God doing through me already?', and 'What does God want to
do through me?' The answer is as likely to be in our life circumstances as in any direct or dramatic call. One level of sharing God's
suffering is to be true to the outward circumstances of our lives as
well as to any particular vocation.

Allowing God to use us in his work of redemption means that
we play our part in 'completing what is lacking in Christ's afflictions
for the sake of his body, that is, the Church'. We no longer have to
feel powerless because we cannot address the whole picture. With
imagination and commitment, when can face the part of the picture
that is ours to address, trusting that God wills the paschal mystery
to be taking place in his world, in us and in our suffering. 'Christianity does not ask us to live in the shadow of the Cross, but in the
fire of its creative action.'[6]

In this prayer is not an option. It is a necessity if we are to
maintain a sense of being part of God's work, involved in God's life
and at one with all who long for this to be the case. *Koinonia* is not
an abstract Greek word but the necessary living reality that under-
pins our lives. There will be suffering in this prayer of seeking union
with God – the suffering of the desert, of christification, deification
– of the fire of God's action in our lives.

IN RESPONSE TO THE NEEDS OF HIS PEOPLE AND THE WORLD

The Beatitudes (Matthew 5: 1–12) are a radical call to share God's
life in reaching beyond ourselves to God and to his world. Listen
again to what Jesus said on the Mountain[7].

Blessed are the poor in spirit, for theirs is the kingdom of heaven

You are blessed . . . You know the presence of God when you are poor in spirit, when you want to possess nothing – not even your own spiritual life – but when you want to give God access to the whole of you for then you have entered God's way. Imagine the Father and the Son and the Holy Spirit . . . how they continually give themselves to each other, how each is pure receptivity to the other, how each is the giver and receiver of grace. It has been said that God is himself only in pouring himself out. The Son too pours himself out on the Father . . . total giving, total poverty. Jesus says to those who would follow him hold onto nothing which God wants of you. Be yourself and reach beyond yourself.

Blessed are those who mourn, for they will be comforted

You are blessed . . . You know the presence of God when you share his heart, when you are not afraid to feel deep within the grief that God feels as he looks at his broken world, at our broken societies, at our broken selves. Blessed are you when you look on the poverty of the world, when you feel deeply the pain of God, the rage of Christ, for then you will pray and you will act in his name and you will be strengthened in His name, by His spirit, the Comforter. Blessed are you when you share God's anger at the suffering of his children and when you share Christ's rage at the apparent absence of God. (Matthew 27: 46)[8]

Blessed are the meek, for they will inherit the earth

You are blessed . . . You know the presence of God when you stand alongside the underdogs of life, the outcasts, the powerless. Like Jesus, they are poor. Blessed are those who are not in too much of a hurry to get things done and know how to wait helpless nailed to their cross. Blessed are those who know when not to wait but to put love into action in real and down to earth ways. Against the odds it is truly they who will inherit God's earth.

Blessed are those who hunger and thirst for righteousness, for they will be filled

You are blessed . . . You know the presence of God when you are passionate for justice on earth, when you long for the justice that can only come from God, when you hunger and thirst for a knowledge of God which will be satisfied not only for you but for all people, the

poor, the children of the world, for the babies of Rwanda and
Sarajevo. Blessed are you for you share God's longing for his world.
You will be filled with God.

Blessed are the merciful, for they will receive mercy

You are blessed . . . You know the presence of God when you know
the faithful love of God and can show it in your love. You are
blessed when you have learnt to be tender-hearted for others and
when you have discovered your forgiveness, when you have learnt
to break cycles of self-centredness by reaching out to others.

Blessed are the pure in heart, for they will see God

You are blessed . . . You know the presence of God when you allow
God continually to renew you in the very depths of your being,
when you allow him to show you his love which has been for you
since he knit you together in your mother's womb. You are blessed
when you know that love and when you allow it to reach out
through you to others. Blessed are you when you are transparent
like clear water – willingly allowing God to see through you, and
allowing others to see God through you.

Blessed are the peacemakers, for they will be called sons of God

You are blessed . . . You know the presence of God when you allow
yourself to find peace within, when you know yourself totally
accepted, totally forgiven, totally loved by God[9] and when you reach
beyond yourself to others in acceptance and love and seek their
peace, their deep peace. Blessed are you when you are so committed
to God that you will consent not only to be taken by him, not
only to be blessed by him but also to suffer for him, for then great
will be your reward. Then, at last you have reached beyond yourself
and reached out for God. You have reached beyond yourself in love
for his world.

Blessed are those who are persecuted because of righteousness, for theirs is the kingdom of heaven

You are blessed when you are prepared to labour with God and
allow him to labour in you that he may bring to birth his new
creation. Blessed are you when you are no longer content with
religion for religion's sake but long only for God's truth, when you
long for the truth of Jesus' life to be the truth of your life, when

you can accept poverty in order to be with the poor Christ, when you will accept insults in order that you may be closer to Jesus in his rejection by people, when all you desire is to be with him . . . when you have the grace to share his resurrection joy.

Blessed are you when people revile you and persecute you and utter all kinds of evil against you on my account. Rejoice and be glad, because your reward is great in heaven, for in the same way they persecuted the prophets who were before you
You are blessed . . . You know the presence of God when you would rather be a clown and a fool for God than be considered wise by those who deal in the standards of a fleeting world. You are blessed when you live so closely to Christ that his life is lived in yours and your life is lived in his.

Your are blessed. You have nothing yet you possess everything . . . you have nothing and yet you know God.

To respond to this call of Christ is to consent to a life of prayer that shows itself in the fibres of our living. There can be no distinction between praying and living for to share God's dynamic is to become holy (Lev 19: 1) – holy in its most generous forms.[10]

IN SEEKING TO RELIEVE THE NEEDS OF OTHERS

We noted[11] that Karl Barth says of God:

> God gives himself, but he does not give himself away . . . He does not cease to be God.[12]

In seeking to relieve the needs of others we seek to give ourselves but not give ourselves away. We cannot serve humanity if we lose our own humanity. The task is to be ourselves and reach beyond ourselves, becoming truly eccentric – out of centre – centred in ourselves in God (truly human) but reaching beyond ourselves. In this way we not only respect ourselves but offer true respect for others for we recognise our connectedness but also our distinctiveness.

Our being willing to share the suffering of others will have practical outcomes but also deeper responses. It cannot be emphasised enough that alleviating suffering is the first task when alleviation is possible and desired. The task of listening to others' stories is another.

The man on the radio was talking about child abuse. He spoke clearly and evenly. When the presenter asked him whether he had been abused himself he quietly told his story – abused by a friend of his father when he was five, by a neighbour when he was nine and by a priest for two years from the age of 14. The presenter asked him how it affected his life now. Again he spoke quietly and evenly saying how it was no longer in his mind every day. He no longer felt he needed to redeem it. He had let it go. But then he talked about how it had been for many years – how he not only knew himself to have been abused but felt he was the abuse.

Here is another level of story not just about what had happened to the man but about the deep darkness of the world. It's a story which reveals how desolation can be transformed into consolation for the man had come to terms with his suffering and was helping others who had been abused, but it also recalls the cost of that.

To listen to such a story and to 'receive it' within oneself is to be touched at a deep level where compassion for the victim and rage at the abuser mingle and where deeper resonances can only be heard by those who dare to seek truth. It may also evoke 'a compassion that includes a certain trouble of mind in the listener at the thought that he could be capable of the same sin'.[13]

In other words the listener becomes aware of the connectedness of the darkness of the world with their own personal darkness. It may be that they would never commit that particular act but know that under stress they could be – have been – capable of other acts of betrayal. This is one side of the deep connectedness of humanity. The other is the practical compassion which makes listening bearable – a gift offered for the sake of the other.

Those who listen professionally and often to such stories pay a heavy cost unless they too have people to whom they can turn. On a purely human level we need the network of relationships that sustains us to be strong if we are to be available to others who need our unconditional positive regard but who are not expected or able, because of their situation, to offer a mutuality of relationship. The experience of this deeply supportive network is the experience of human *koinonia*.[14]

There is however another level of *koinonia* where all of this is recognised as being held in Christ in God. At this level we join the struggle between all that is life-giving and good and all that is destructive. It is the ground on which intercessory prayer takes place at a deep level.

Intercession is an indispensable aspect of the apostolate of prayer, and the great awesome challenge of it is that it is the point of prayer at which we stand with Christ in tension: it is there that the reconciling love and power of God meets the pain and suffering of the world, of individuals and of ourselves. It is at this point that we are ourselves most vulnerable. Interceding is not reminding God of his duties, it is taking a step towards the heart of the world.[15]

In such intercession the paschal mystery finds its reflection in the human heart. It can feel like carrying some of the 'darkness' of the world and at times we may be aware of carrying some of the darkness for a particular situation or person. It is a privileged way of prayer – a share in the sufferings of Christ.

OFFERING THE SUFFERING OF OUR HUMANITY TO HIM, AND BEARING WHATEVER COMES OUR WAY AS A RESULT OF DISCIPLESHIP

It may be helpful to make the distinction between *the call of God to us to be the unique person that we are* living in the situation in which we live and *the call of God to a particular area of serving others* – whether through caring for the physical needs of others or the call to deep intercession which itself is immensely costly.

Obviously at some levels the distinction is a false one but it helps us understand how God may be calling us and how that call may incur suffering. It also helps us see the need for discernment if we are to discriminate between suffering that should be borne and suffering that should be alleviated or avoided.[16]

Francis de Sales, a seventeenth-century mystical writer, believed that God's will, though ultimately a single will, was known to us in various forms. He suggested two distinct forms – what we may call 'God's signified will' and God's inherent will'.[17] God's signified will is known through prayer, discussion with others, and inspiration. When it has not been received in this way then it is made by human reasoning and choices but once decided upon then this too should be acted upon as God's will.[18] God's signified will requires our active consent. God's inherent will finds expression in the concrete realities of our life. It is in the situation which we face with all its limitations, gifts, joys and suffering – 'where one finds oneself, one's particular situation, is also revelatory of the divine will and must be taken into account and lived with creatively if one is to be truly responsive to the unique will of God.'[19] It is emphatically not the case that God wills us to be in a place of suffering. God's inherent will is discovered as we live as creatively as we can with the reality of who we are, where we are, when we are, with our finitude and with our real responsibilities to ourselves and to others.

> God is found wherever one finds oneself. . . It is not that one is God's will and the other isn't until an impasse causes one to change one's shape of divine will. It is rather that living *between* the two wills – maintaining a creative tension that refuses to limit God to one expression or the other – is in itself more consonant with the immensity and simplicity of the essence of a God whose wholeness can never be contained in any one part of creation.[20]

This view of God's will means that everyone is living within the will of God – within his creative and redemptive embrace. Some will be clear about a 'signified will' but those who live strongly with a sense of God's 'inherent will' are living fully their calling. The danger, sometimes, is that those who have a clear sense of the 'signified will of God' sometimes forsake God's inherent will that they be also truly the person God made.

In essence these are aspects of a single divine will and the suffering that comes our way cannot be clearly distinguished but may relate to either or both.

Praying about our own suffering is an important aspect of having compassion for ourselves and so being available for others. It is not just about taking things to the cross and leaving them there. It is likely that we cannot let things go until we have worked through them. It may well be that rather than leaving things at the cross we may need to carry them with Christ for a while until they have lost their power to inflict more wounds on us.

Suddenly life seemed different and yet everything was the same. He had carried that particular pain for a long time and every time he went on retreat he seemed to have to face it again. The person who was alongside him suggested that he might let go of it and for the next day he struggled to do so. Then she suggested that rather than let go in the sense of trying to escape it he should allow it to be held in God so that God might transform it and use it, and maybe, in time, set him free from it. That made more sense and it took several years but gradually he came to see that he no longer carried that particular pain and it no longer damaged

his relationships with others. He discovered that his greatest weakness was
a hidden strength. He wrote:

> *There is no other way . . . Have on your heart the one word which for*
> *you calls on the mystery which is God and as you enter the wilderness*
> *which is you, speak that word so that God may speak His Word in you.*
> *Let everything that we see, hear, think, feel, taste and touch draw us*
> *back to the centre of our being where God dwells . . . when we are drawn*
> *away let us gently bring ourselves back, gently so that we may hear the*
> *faintest whisper of the voice of love and when our gaze is drawn to*
> *the areas of our lives which seem to threaten us, we can let go of the*
> *fear that leads to shame, and look rather with love, look through to*
> *the Father and wait, stay still until it is his time to do what he must do –*
> *pour himself out in love that you, that I, might be healed.*

How might we consent to live between these two wills? What
does it mean in practice? What holds them together is longing love –
the love of desire to do God's will. Sheila Cassidy writes:

> This time I write of the intangible, the unknowable: of what I
> understand as encounter with God. The experience is one which
> has changed my life in that it has given me a sort of carnal
> knowledge, a gut level conviction of an all powerful, loving
> God. This conviction is, I believe, the greatest gift that I bring
> to my work, enabling me to sustain somehow, those who are
> afraid and in pain.
>
> My particular encounter with God happened in the context
> of solitary confinement in prison – but it could just as well have
> been after a major accident, an illness or bereavement. The
> essence of the situation was that it was an experience of strip-
> ping and of powerlessness, which made me more, more open,
> to the presence of God.
>
> It happened like this. After I had been arrested and interro-
> gated by the secret police for treating a wounded revolutionary,
> I was moved from the torture centre to another prison and
> placed in solitary confinement. Here, left to my own devices
> and with the constant harassment of the interrogation behind
> me I found that, for the first time since my arrest, I had sufficient
> emotional and intellectual space to manoeuvre, to choose what
> to do. My immediate inclination was to scream out to God for
> help, to batter spiritually on the bars of my cage, begging to be
> released. Surely, I who was planning to devote my life to him
> as a nun, must be specially loved and able to ask his favour?

Then a very curious thing suggested itself to me: while I knew that it was quite right and proper that I should besiege heaven with my prayers to be released, an even better way would be to hold out my hands to God, not in supplication but in offering. I would say, not 'Please let me out', but, 'Here I am Lord, take me, I trust you, do with me what you will'. In my powerlessness and captivity there remained to me one freedom: I could abandon myself into the hands of God... So for the next three weeks I struggled to let go the strings of my life, to hand myself over to God. It was not a once and forever dramatic gesture, but a long and terrible struggle... This option for abandonment is available to all who find themselves trapped by circumstance and is the means by which the imprisoned can transcend their bonds. Like a bird in a cage they can learn to live within the confines of their prison and find, to their surprise, that they still have a song to sing.[21]

There are echoes here of Brian Keenan's belief that there are always choices. Accepting the reality of a situation is the only way in which real choices can be made, but this does not mean one accepts the situation should be that way. Acceptance may be the point from which one passionately works for change, but it is the place where the situation may be offered to God, the place where 'the imprisoned can transcend their bonds', and reach beyond suffering.

SUFFERING, LIFE AND PRAYER

In this chapter we have explored what it means to share the suffering of Christ in the reality of our lives and in the life of the world. We have recognised the need to face facts – something to which we return in the final chapter. But we long to do more than face facts – we long to reach beyond them. It is to this that we now turn.

10

REACHING BEYOND SUFFERING

Stop all the clocks, cut off the telephone,
Prevent the dog from barking with a juicy bone,
Silence the pianos and with muffled drum
Bring out the coffin, let the mourners come.

Let aeroplanes circle moaning overhead
Scribbling on the sky the message He Is Dead,
Put crepe bows round the white necks of the public doves,
Let traffic policemen wear black cotton gloves.

He was my North, my South, my East and West,
My working week and my Sunday rest,
My noon, my midnight, my talk, my song;
I thought that love would last forever: I was wrong.

The stars are not wanted now: put out every one;
Pack up the moon and dismantle the sun;
Pour away the ocean and sweep up the wood;
For nothing now can ever come to any good.[1]

As Auden conveys so movingly in this famous poem, there is no escaping the reality that suffering can be horrendous, and we can be so paralysed by it that we can think or feel or say nothing. It can truly seem to be a dead end. Once we can find some distance from it we can begin to reach beyond suffering either to alleviate or work through it.

In this chapter we explore the possibility of reaching beyond suffering, with particular reference to St. John of the Cross. H.A. Williams writes:

> It is the nature of human privations and sufferings of all kinds to feel like dead ends. But human suffering, the more of a dead-end it feels like, the more it is an invitation to join in Christ's

sufferings, and in Him to help bring light and life and healing and liberty to mankind.[2]

TRANSFORMATION AND REDEMPTION

There are two aspects of the way we might use suffering in the light of Christ's suffering. There is the possibility of transformation so that Easter comes from a Good Friday experience. This is often the transformation of a person or an outlook on life, and not a transformation of events. Suffering is still suffering though the person afflicted may become a source of healing for others. Transformation may also happen when pain and suffering lead to an intense resolve to change the situation in which suffering was inevitable.

There is also the belief that suffering offered to God is redemptive for others if not for the people immediately involved, paradoxically becomes redemptive for them too.[3] Reaching beyond suffering involves both these approaches.

OPEN TO CHANGE

To risk this kind of transformation we need to be open to change. It requires us to abandon ourselves to the situation and to the embrace of God beyond it; to fully embrace the Christian life including its call to repentance (Gk. *metanoia*), deification, christ-ification[4], and the total change of *Conversatio morum*[5]. It requires us to turn away from what is not God and to turn to God, 'becoming like him in his death, if somehow I may attain the resurrection from the dead' (Philippians 3: 11). It is a process which is God's initiative but which requires our response. It is a process of encounter with God in all his manifestations and encounter with the failing power of our illusions about ourselves. It is a breaking down of idols, a constant letting go, a radical discipleship which longs for intimacy with Christ though often does not *feel* that longing. It is a path which offers little felt security and which depends completely on God. The path sometimes requires our active participation and at other times our passive acceptance of what God is doing – not in the sense of doing nothing but in the Christ-like sense of creative acceptance.[6] There will be times of warmth and light but there will also be dry and uninteresting times. Both are necessary to the path. St John of the Cross highlights that these arid and sometimes painful times are actually not a sign of the absence of God but of his deeper transforming presence. For John there is a difference between suffering *per se* and the kind of suffering which is part of what he calls 'Night'.

NIGHT

> This is what turns pain into night: grieve, address what can be addressed, do not condone that sin that may be causing the situation; but trust that the Father holds this situation in his hands, and will turn it to blessing.[7]

In the last chapter we made the distinction between the inherent will of God and the signified will of God. We noted that this is not a clear-cut distinction but can help us to see where suffering is coming from – from our facticity, relationships and environment or, in a more specific way, from following Christ. Whatever the cause of our suffering, John's understanding of 'Night' is that we can allow God to use our suffering to make himself known. Even if our suffering has nothing to do with our Christian discipleship it can still be offered to God and become transformed.

'Night' for John has three aspects. It involves suffering of the kind that turns life upside down, suffering that leaves us bewildered. It involves God breaking into the situation. Iain Matthew uses a beautiful image:

> As tent canvas drenched in rain needs only to be touched for the water to seep in, so a universe drenched in an outpoured Spirit needs only a touch, but it does need a touch, for the healing Spirit to seep in.[8]

For John of the Cross the fundamental belief is that God is universally and actively present in his creation. It is not that sometimes God is closer than at others. He is always seeking to make himself known to us. He needs space – space that we make for him and space that we allow him to make in us. Night therefore involves an inflow of God. Night also involves a creative response from us – an openness to God.

John does not deny that pain and suffering are terrible; he does not suggest that we feel God's presence in it. He affirms without doubt that God is present but that the pain is pain and the mess we experience is a mess. He writes:

> What the sorrowing soul feels most is the conviction that God

has rejected it, and with abhorrence cast it into darkness . . . it feels very vividly indeed the shadow of death, the sighs of death, and the sorrows of hell. . . Such persons also feel forsaken and despised by creatures, particularly by their friends . . . it feels . . . this terrible undoing in its very substance . . . it becomes uncertain of any remedy.[9]

There is no denying the suffering of the night. As Iain Matthew puts it:

Night is taking us, then, not to some soiree for a self-preoccupied elite, but to the heart of the world's suffering. It declares the world's wounds to be spaces through which God may graciously enter.[10]

Night is not something to be glorified in itself. It is what night achieves in us when we consent to God's action that is glorious. Night takes us out of control of the situation. It takes us out of ourselves, so that we reach beyond ourselves to God. Our suffering carves out this space in us that God may fill it. We are set free to view our suffering differently and to respond differently, not by ignoring its pain and agony but when it is possible, by reaching beyond the pain to God and to creative engagement with life. In my own life such a time of suffering led me to a prayer of consent:

Father,
from stone you fashioned flesh
and, in a twinkle gave it breath.
I had no choice.
It was your 'yes'
But now I give consent
bear me again, give birth to me
that I may birth your Son for those I serve.

Shape me by the blows and joys of life
Chisel me intricately as once you knit me, nurtured me in the
    womb.
Smooth me gently with your love as once you quietened my
    baby soul.
Shape me, conform me, to your Son.
carve out in me a great space for yourself,
my living heart
that those who come to me may find
your love, your compassion. . .

None of this helps us when we are going through the night; it doesn't help the struggle.

> John does not want to say, 'It's all right, you see, because this is the explanation'. He wants to say, 'It's not all right, it's a mess. But you are not alone in this. God is present in this. Now is not the time to lose faith in him.[11]

Understanding this level of pain, and seeing it in Jesus crucified, it should not surprise us that Christians identify strongly with the crucified one. John writes:

> I will go seek my bride
> and take upon myself
> her weariness and labors
> in which she suffers so,
> and that she may have life
> I will die for her,
> and lifting her out of that deep,
> I will restore her to you.[12]

In this poem lies the paschal mystery once more: death gives way to restoration, and God is on the inside of our pain in order to transform us into himself.

This is at the heart of the mystery of night. The apparent absence of God may be his transforming presence and the great emptiness we feel may be precisely that space in us which God may fill with his fullness. For John *nada* (nothing) makes space for *todo* (everything). God on the inside of our pain may not have experienced in Christ the exact circumstances of our pain but he has experienced the depth of pain, especially the pain that gnaws at the spirit. He suffers it with us and in us.

GOD'S APPARENT ABSENCE

The opening of the Spiritual Canticle, a poem written by John of the Cross when he was held prisoner in Toledo for nine months, says it all:

> Where have you hidden,
> Beloved, and left me moaning?

Where does God hide when atrocities are happening in the world, when creation reveals not its warmth but its wildness, when relationships turn sour and love seems impossible, when bereavement takes the puzzle of our lives and scatters all the pieces on the floor. Where is God sleeping then? (Psalm 44: 23) Why is he hiding his face? (Psalms 10: 11, 13: 1, 27: 9).[13]

Why then is he absent when we need him most? Why was he absent for Jesus on the Cross? As Moltmann puts it, 'Who is God in the cross of Christ who is abandoned by God?'[14] In chapter 8 we quoted Simone Weil:

> Because nobody else could do it, he [God] himself went to the greatest possible distance, the infinite distance. This infinite distance between God and God, this supreme tearing apart, this agony beyond all others, this marvel of love, is the crucifixion.

St John of the Cross too sees that Jesus has gone this ultimate distance:

> at the moment of his death he was certainly annihilated in his soul, without any consolation or relief... This was the most extreme abandonment... And by it he accomplished the most marvellous work of his whole life... That is he brought about the reconciliation and union of the human race with God through grace.[15]

Jesus was reduced to nothing (*nada*) and so received for us everything (*todo*). Jesus went the ultimate distance and is with us when we travel that way. John knows that what will help us in our pain is not illusory promises of relief but the reality that we are not alone – that God's presence, though not felt, is unquestionable.

To live by this belief is to reach beyond ourselves in encounter with God. It is to trust-without-strings. It may feel like death and a loss of identity.

HUMANITY

William Johnston describes this state succinctly:

> this... is a time of death and resurrection. The framework that upheld one's life collapses leaving one adrift on a sea of insecurity. But in the midst of this turmoil comes a call... One is called to something new.[16]

Such an experience can feel immensely threatening but it is not God's intention to destroy us or weaken our humanity. He wants to set us free to be truly human. The 'night' that John describes, though it may involve intense suffering, is a night that opens up to a greater love not only for God and from God but for others as we are set free from all that enslaves us and ties us down. John describes such attachments like a bird being held down by a cord.[17] It does not matter whether the cord is thin or thick. It still ties the bird down. Once the cord is cut the bird takes flight. So we may take flight as the attachments are taken from us. Nobody describes it better than William Johnston:

> When with tears and anguish and pain you have said goodbye to everything you will find that you have lost nothing. You have not said goodbye to your friends: you have said goodbye to clinging and attachment to your friends. You have not said goodbye to memories: you have said goodbye to clinging and attachment to memories. You have not said goodbye to the good things of this world: you have said goodbye to clinging and attachment to the good things of this world. You have not said goodbye to knowing and rationality: you have said goodbye to clinging and attachment to knowing and rationality. You have not said goodbye to doctrines and dogmas: you have said goodbye to clinging and attachment to doctrines and dogmas. And so for all good things.[18]

The night, then, is not an attempt to reduce us to nothing, though it feels like nothing, but an attempt to make space for everything – for a love that is free – for God. It is not a diminishment of our humanity but a fulfilment of it.

The theory is fine. With hindsight, the practice is also fine, but when the night is in full force and the storm is raging, the windows of our lives are rattling in their frames, the tiles falling off our roof and we wonder whether the wolf will blow us down like the home of the three little pigs, theory doesn't actually hold us together. Only God can do that and longing love – his and ours. Only longing love holds together the abyss of love and the abyss of emptiness. What helps us more than anything is to be aware of the smallest desire for God and to know that our longing for God holds a powerful secret – 'God is on the inside of our longing'[19] and if we can refuse to panic and hold steady we might become aware of his shadow within and gradually aware of him, even in the darkness.

Iain Matthew writes that God is continually pressing in to make himself known. In darkness then it is not the absence of God that causes us difficulty 'but the *way* he is present.'[20] St John of the Cross talks of God being present but 'hidden'.[21]

It is important when facing the darkness to be clear about where our identity lies – to know where we are rooted, even when we *feel* unrooted. One aspect of our identity is that God is already, by virtue of our creation, within all of us and by virtue of our baptism within those who have responded to Christ. 'Your life is hidden with Christ in God' (Colossians 3: 3).

Our identity is shaped too by our association with others – hence the absolute importance of *koinonia* – and not only with those who think like us, but also with those who are very different from us. In encountering the darkness of the world, in ourselves, in others and in the structures of society we face this 'clash of contraries'[22] and are led to discover more of where our true identity lies.

The prophet Jeremiah and the person of Jesus have their identity firmly rooted in God. They identify and connect with the people they serve but are also distinct from them so they can, for example, both love Jerusalem and stand against Jerusalem because of that love. This connectedness and distinction is an important part of identity. We are identified both with the crucified and risen Christ and with what is furthest from God.[23]

THRESHOLDS

Becoming aware of our identity is a process which will take us over many thresholds as we are taken beyond ourselves by circumstance and have to redefine our identity. For John of the Cross his time in prison became a major threshold when he was taken out of himself. Iain Matthew writes, 'He had been hauled beyond the threshold of his own resources'.[24] Thresholds in our life have that effect. They take us from the security that we know and open up freedom and insecurity. They make us unsure of ourselves and so we become an enigma both to ourselves and others. Like Lazurus coming from the tomb crossing a threshold may be a call to life but it is also a call to risk and to risk everything. It may well be that at the threshold there is a time to pause, to wait, to let things unfold in the providence of God. Indeed waiting at the threshold in the darkness may be long but we can cross it only when the time is right. It is God's initiative rather than ours.[25]

JOURNEY WITHOUT A MAP

Passing through arid ground and crossing thresholds is not only painful but unclear. The darkness can be absolute with no way to discern what the next step will be. There may be no sense of inner growth at all, just a faithful hope that God is working at depth, beyond our ability to sense. The experience of darkness itself will have made the map by which we had been living useless in part if not completely.

Without a map one can only trust that the guide – God – is infallible when we cannot see where we are going. What we can do, and what those who advise us may help us to do is not exhaust ourselves trying to make a path or take short-cuts which do not aid our journey. This journey is about being carried not by events but by God. The task is simply to stay faithful even in the darkness, though the word 'simply' carries a whole weight of struggle, pain and suffering. Let's not pretend otherwise.

But the guide is infallible and has gone through darkness himself. And the energy we need for the journey comes not from ourselves but from the future – the new life and hope that speaks of the presence of a God who remains hidden, a God who has himself been wounded, and reaches in healing to our wounds.

PRESENCE

Late Have I loved you, O beauty ever ancient, ever new!
    Late, have I loved you.
And behold you were within, and I without, and without I
    sought you.
    And deformed, I ran after those forms of beauty you have
      made.
You were with me, and I was not with you, those things held
    me back
      from you, things whose only being was to be in you.
    You called, you cried, and you broke through my
    deafness.
You illumined, you shone, and you chased away my
    blindness.
      You became fragrant and I inhaled and sighed for you.
        I tasted and now hunger and thirst for you.
      You touched me and I burned for your embrace.

St Augustine's prayer speaks powerfully of the presence of God within us. This is John's vision too – that we find the presence of God not outside ourselves, but within.

> ... in the midst of these dark and loving afflictions, the soul feels a certain companionship and an interior strength; these so fortify and accompany it that when this weight of anxious darkness passes, the soul often feels alone, empty and weak.[26]

Anthony de Mello describes this experience in prayer:

> If they avoid this evil and persevere in the exercise of prayer and expose themselves, in blind faith, to the emptiness, the darkness, the idleness, the nothingness, they will gradually discover, at first in small flashes, later in a more permanent fashion, that there is a glow in the darkness, that the emptiness mysteriously fills their heart, that the idleness is full of God's activity, that in the nothingness their being is recreated and shaped anew ... and all this in a way that they cannot describe either to themselves or others.[27]

This is the essence of any understanding of the night – that ultimately night is about the presence of God, even though that presence is not easy to understand and eludes our grasp. It cannot be described; it is beyond words. There is no way we can possess God, except he give us himself. The longing and desire of God is to do precisely that – to be our God and we his people. John of the Cross puts it this way:

> for he would make himself
> wholly like them,
> and he would come to them
> and dwell with them;
> and God would be man
> and man would be God,
> and he would walk with them
> and eat and drink with them;
> and he himself would be
> with them continually
> until the consummation
> of this world.[28]

This is not a passive presence but an active one. God looks on us with love and in that gaze we are changed. This gaze of love is the essence of any trust that God may be carrying us through the darkness. St Ignatius suggests that before praying we spend the space of an 'Our Father' considering how God gazes at us.[29] Commenting on this Brian Grogan writes, 'God loves me as a person, wishes to give me all possible gifts, God included.'[30]

So God looks at us and we at him even in the darkness:

> Then the gaze into the face of Jesus of Nazareth is changed into the face to face vision of God, even if both the encounter with Jesus and the consequent vision of God only make that presence fully known when the confinement of our poor body is split open by death'[31]

WOUNDS

God is wounded by love and the crucified one bears the marks of those wounds. Our woundedness cannot separate us from God and we have no need to hide our wounds or deal with them before we come to God. In the meeting of our wounds with his, healing comes.

In fact the root of our woundedness is often to be found in our sense of powerlessness, meaninglessness, isolation and lack of love. To these wounds God ministers. He merely invites us to recognise our need and become receptive to him. The wounds themselves are the means by which God finds the space to enter. Into our poverty and emptiness comes the fullness of God. It is so often when we cry out to God in searing pain that we let go of ourselves and let God enter in a new way.

During the time I was looking after Jackie I came to prayer exhausted, tense and angry. Prayer would not happen. Then I looked at a cross, reached for my pen, and wrote:

> Pain,
> Perpetual pain,
> Aching, slogging, grieving,
> feeling,
> piercing, future blinding
> round embracing,
> isolating,
> oneness
> loneness
> weary sadness making.
>
> Pain of watching,

waiting
nothing certain
one year, two years
time is breaking over
day by day
and holding in its grasp
our lives and loss.

Pain of never winning
not improving
slowly waiting
for the end that will be no end
but start again of grieving
paining,
pining
further anger
sadness.

Pain of being rendered helpless.
Nothing cures
though love can ease the time
of days and nights of
help me, turn me, lift me
feed me,
touch me softly, giving
hopeful love's embrace.

Is this empty
Pain of inner man?
Analgesics cannot touch
this deeper hurt.
Can it covered be by
alcohol's soft dream
or drugs high lift?

Is there in the hurt
endured,
a glimpse of Christ
hanging, waiting, paining
on the tree.
Is this pain a part
of when our Lord
is crossing me?

No answer have I
Only this I say
that when I look at him
He is with me.[32]

REACHING BEYOND OURSELVES

In all of this there is a reaching beyond ourselves in prayer and love, or being taken beyond the threshold by circumstances. Either way we can either consent to the loving, yet hidden presence of God, or we can run from the experience and run from God. Meanwhile, we do everything in our power to alleviate unnecessary suffering in others and in ourselves. The 'night' is that suffering which cannot be alleviated. Spirituality is no excuse for making ourselves victims or martyrs unnecessarily.

11

SUFFERING AND SILENCE

Listen . . .
To the fragile feelings,
    not the clashing fury . . .
To the quiet sounds,
    not the loud clamour . . .
To the steady heartbeat,
    not the noisy confusion . . .
To the hidden voices,
    not the obvious chatter . . .
To the deep harmonies,
    not the surface discord . . .
Listen to the language of your wounds
    and your love.[1]

A young man who died of AIDS wrote:

> Affliction, pain especially . . . can be obliterating. It can take
> away the desire, the sheer ability to do anything but suffer. At
> other times though it powerfully peels away pretence and
> shallow evasion and confronts us with the sharp and deep
> questions.[2]

Affliction takes us into levels of suffering that are completely
beyond words. It is only later, should we survive, that we can begin
to articulate the silence. Those around us may discover that silence
and a loving presence is all that can be offered. Words may feel like
bullets piercing the afflicted with more pain – 'when God tears great
gaps in our lives we should not try to fill them with words'.[3]
Yet at other times words are angels of healing bringing exactly what
we need and silence itself would be destructive. There is 'a time to
keep silent and a time to speak' (Ecclesiastes 3: 7). In this chapter
we explore the nature of silence in prayer and in suffering.

THE SILENCE OF GOD

Jesus' forsakenness on the Cross leads him to cry out to God 'My God, my God, why have you forsaken me?' (Matthew 27.46). The psalm that has entered his soul through prayer now speaks from his soul in desperation. The psalm continues, 'Why are you so far from helping me, from the words of my groaning? O my God, I cry by day but you do not answer; and by night but find no rest'. (Psalm 22, 1, 2).

It is this 'silence of absence' which is so painful. It feeds our fears and fantasies, our self-doubts and self-accusations (for example, Job 29 – 31). St John of the Cross writes that 'the soul's greatest suffering in the trials of this night is the anguish of thinking it has lost God and been abandoned by him . . . the soul is aware that the greatest suffering it experiences in these trials is this fear'[4].

Archie Hill describes his experience of entering a relationship with a woman who had a disabled child, Barry:

> Who is this puppet-master that men call God, who has no guts to face me? Who is this craven coward who has the reputed magic to fashion sprawling galaxies and universes, yet ruined the personal universe of my wife's son? Locked him into a fixed position then sucked away his inner-atmosphere; created a part-universe only, a poor broken toy. I stand here knowing that the perfections of mankind come about in spite of this God, and the imperfections because of his neglect. I stand here and I know that my wife and son have suffered more than Christ ever did, beyond his capability to bear such pain, beyond his capacity for it.[5]

No wonder a father rages against God because his wife's son had been born disabled. No words can meet his rage. His experience of God cannot be changed by intellectual argument, only by an experience of present love.

Hesitant, careful words may come later about the love he has felt for the boy and for the boy's mother, about the love he has seen the mother lavish on the boy. 'I, who never knew for so many long wasted years what love was, have learned the true richness of what love is. Have learned from my wife and Barry.'[6]

None of this denies the pain and affliction but it changes the 'feel' and the meaning. It speaks of God being within the love, and of God sharing the suffering *from the inside*. It takes as fact that suffering happens with no attempt to justify it or explain it. It emphasises a true theology.

It is important to have a sound theology if one is to be alongside those who suffer – a theology that focuses on the love of God, that affirms that suffering is not a punishment from God, that affirms that God suffers with us and in us and wishes to relieve suffering and transform our suffering or ability to live with that suffering. A sound theology recognises the reality of suffering but does not claim it to be a better spiritual path or a necessary one unless it cannot be legitimately alleviated. It points beyond suffering to other values and aspirations, not as a denial or avoidance but as a way of working with suffering. It demands careful listening, wise sensitivity, and a sense of humour. Above all it demands a paschal overview – the holding together of loss and gain, death and resurrection – not necessarily articulated but lived in love.[7]

THE 'SILENCE' OF PRESENCE

It is this great absence
that is like a presence, that compels
me to address it without hope
of a reply. It is a room I enter
from which someone has just
gone, the vestibule for the arrival
of one who has not yet come.
I modernise the anachronism

of my language, but he is no more here
than before. Genes and molecules
have no more power to call
him up than the incense of the Hebrews

at their altars. My equations fail
as my words do. What resource have I
other than the emptiness without him of my whole
being, a vacuum he may not abhor?[8]

R. S. Thomas writes of this other silence of God – the silence that is in fact a presence though that presence be like a fleeting glimpse.

His are the echoes
We follow, the footprints he has just
left. We put our hands in

His side hoping to find
it warm. We look at people
and places as though he had looked
At them, too; but miss the reflection.[9]

This silence is hopeful. It is the silence of the two who had met Jesus on the Emmaus Road, seeing who he was when he broke the bread but then finding him gone. This is the silence after we have listened to a great piece of music and been captivated by it as its beauty enabled us to transcend ourselves. It is a silence of love and life; a place where we may reflect on what we have been shown and learn from that reflection. It is not just the silence that follows a revelation of love and life. It is the silence of anticipation – a silence which gains its ambience from what is to come rather than what has been, a silence of hope, a silence that is shaped by the meaning and weight we give to a situation.

These different kinds of silence have echoes in our relationship with ourselves, with others and with God in prayer.

ALONENESS AND LONELINESS

He silent and angry,
she silent and afraid, each looking
out the cab windows,
he to the left, she to the right,
both dressed for winter, driving
somewhere neither wants to go.[10]

Loneliness can be most focused not when we are alone but when we are with others in a silence of hostility and fear. It is another 'silence of absence'. But loneliness can be an intolerable burden in whatever guise it takes us. There can be a destructive silence of loneliness, or there can be a healing and life-giving silence of being 'all one' – alone. The silence of being all one is the silence that comes having passed through the silence of loneliness in a life-giving way.

The silence of loneliness, of empty absence, is surrounded by fear. It can feel as if we have been forgotten by everybody, that our isolation is complete and our identity unsteady. In extreme situations it feels like being wrapped in the coldness of non-being. It saps all our energy and makes taking interest in life seem futile. Should the silence also be as a result of the rejection of others, or is perceived as such, the feelings of fear of annihilation are even stronger. Such

silence is no longer a means of communication – even with ourselves. It is unhealthy. It is a suffering which needs to be alleviated.

It is perhaps because we know that silence has this potential
that many people fill silence with incessant music, a diary filled to
exhaustion, or a ringing telephone. But there is another silence of
presence, the silence of communication. This silence can help us
come to terms with ourselves and know ourselves and gaze at
ourselves not with sentimental softness but with a realistic and life-
giving compassion.

A few years after my wife died I went on a course which included
a three-day retreat. I had done my grieving and I was expecting a
fairly smooth time. In fact, I still had a lesson to learn. It came to
me during the retreat in several ways, but most strongly in a dream.
The dream made clear in a vivid and memorable way that I was
avoiding my own needs but continuing to try to meet the needs of
everyone else. Looking back I realise that while Jackie was ill it
almost had to be that way. It was a way of coping. My dream, in
which I watched myself burning in a fire, brought home to me the
need to have compassion for myself, to recognise my needs and
address them. It was a painful lesson, one summed up well by
Martin Israel:

> underneath there is the unfulfilled child longing for recognition
> and comfort. Until it is acknowledged there can never be an
> effective communication with myself; until I can communicate
> fully with my inner depths, I will not be able to relate properly
> to anyone else . . . The fact is that until one is at home in oneself,
> one will never be at home in the world.[11]

Unless we can live with our own silence it is unlikely that we
shall be comfortable in company when others are silent and will try
to fill that silence with unnecessary and random conversation.
Martin Israel, writing about his experience of being a hospital
patient, speaks of visitors who:

> came ostensibly to cheer me up and support me, but . . . they
> could not give me any peace. [A visitor] should be in a good
> mood before arriving, also remembering to practise *periods of
> unobtrusive silence*.[12] (my italics)

When we can live with our own silence we can dare to be silent
with others, offering not the silence of rejection but 'unobtrusive
silence', 'communicative silence'[13], or words which come from a

heart of love, spoken carefully, gently, though sometimes challeng-
ingly into the silence.

The alternative, as I discovered during a period of deep depression,
can feel like being pierced by bullets:[14]

> Holy God,
> Insubstantial one,
> feather on the breath of my being,
> let me cherish your presence.
>
> What had held me together,
> held no more.
> Meanings and explanations,
> understandings and passions
> all gone.
> Depression they called it.
> What a wimp of a word![15]
>
> Caged into my stillness,
> somnambulant rage[16]
> pinning me down.
> My inscape, a void.
> Pain glancing me,
> hardly perceived
> but still piercing.
> Why had it beaten me so,
> why cowered me into
> this overcast cave?
>
> And words which at first,
> could not touch me
> became, as I wakened, artillery fire –
> too much, too much to bear.
>
> My soul refuses all comfort
> yet needed you there.[17]
> Perverse in its longings
> yet knowing that
> walking, too soon, from the dark
> was not healing.
>
> And you, insubstantial one,
> whistling of a gentle air[18]
> drew me to wait in the darkness,

in hell not despairing[19],
till freedom should come.[20]

WAITING IN DARKNESS

The poem illustrates the power of words to hurt rather than help. It points out the truth that there are times when we have to be content to wait in the darkness. The most painful realisation can be knowing that walking too soon from the dark was not healing. Unless we learn from the darkness the chances are that our efforts to avoid it will be wasted. Though we may cover it up for a while it will still have power over us until we listen to the language of our wounds and our love. Here we may need the help of others to listen with us and for us so that healing may come.

> The archer with time
> as his arrow – has he broken
> his strings that the rainbow
> is so quiet over our village?
>
> Let us stand, then, in the interval
> of our wounding, till the silence
> turns golden and love is
> a moment eternally overflowing.[21]

The words, though true, are too smooth to hear when one is held in the grip of uncertainty and fear that waiting can become. The experience can seem unbearable so that the emptiness and sense of non-being encourages us to do something, anything, rather than stay in this time of dark waiting, whatever its cause.

What sustains us at such times is the sense of the presence of others even if only in communicative silence, and the belief, for some, in the presence of God even in his seeming absence. Above all what draws us forward is saying 'Yes' to life and 'Yes' to our true selves:

> Kierkegaard 'points out the most common despair is to be in despair at not choosing, or willing, to be oneself, but that the deepest form of despair is to choose to be another than himself. On the other hand 'the will to be that self which one truly is, is indeed the opposite of despair' and this choice is the deepest responsibility of man.[22]

To stay in the darkness and struggle with our fears and fantasies can feel like walking through fire and fire is risky stuff. Fire consumes. It can destroy. To enter fire is to risk everything. There are no half measures. In the words of T.S. Eliot, 'We only live, only suspire, consumed by either fire or fire.'[23] We give our life either to God's consuming fire or to the fire of life without God. It doesn't sound much of a choice. And yet it is a choice between nothingness for its own sake, or the nothingness that leads to the fullness of God – to be consumed by nothing or to be consumed by love. It is only when we trust in the love beyond the nothingness that it is safe to enter the fire, or to entrust the fire that takes us to God. It is only love that calls us like the butterfly to be stripped of our skin, to stand skinless in our own pain and inadequacy. Without love it is not possible. 'Things fall apart, the centre cannot hold' (Yeats)[24]. And the love is in the fire. Nobody describes it better than St John of the Cross. At times in the spiritual journey the fire can feel aggressive – 'like fire burning into wood, first making it sputter and steam, blacken and crackle, until the wood itself becomes flame. But whether the flame is purifying or glorifying, it is the same "fire of love" that is approaching, entering'.[25]

When we ask the spirit to come, to kindle a fire of love, are we not asking that the events of life which strike us and shape us may be the means by which the wounds of love are deepened and the veils between us and God torn down? Torn at first but at times caught up in the flame of love which is the spirit, pierced by nothing but longing love, and that God's longing as well as ours? Isn't this the fire, that we are able to let God surrender himself to us, and we warmed by his love, so surrender ourselves to him? But all this implies difficult and painful waiting – holding the tensions of our pain and suffering until healing comes. Again, I am reflecting on my own experience:

> A violin note hangs in the air,
> the string vibrates with life
> though its cause is for
> an instant gone-
> the touch of bow
> the caress that brought life
> no longer, for an instant there
> And that is how I feel . . .
>
> Aware of the bow that gives me life
> but in the darkness

no longer, for the moment,
able to feel its touch
and so alone
though not alone.

And though my life
vibrates within
without its cause
I know I fade away.

The bow is life and love . . .
when will the bow touch me again?
Is this silence part of the melody . . .
a measured length to hold the notes in place,
a silence that prevents harmony
disintegrating into chaos?

I cannot tell.
It cannot yet be clear
and like a silent string
I can but wait.

All around me other strings
are humming,
trumpets blaring,
horns harrumphing..
and yet I am still . . . the tension
that makes me me
no use at all without the bow
that turns my tension into song
my being taut into a melody.
How long, O Lord, how long?

Sometimes, of course, healing does not come in the way we would choose.

WAITING

Whilst ice-bound in the Arctic, the Norwegian explorer Nansen wrote:

> I long to return to life . . . the years are passing here . . . Oh! at times this inactivity crushes the soul; one's life seems dark as the winter night outside; there is sunlight upon no part of it

except the past and the far, far distant future. I feel as though I
must break through this deadness.[26]

This is a superb description of how it can feel to be caught in a
time of waiting, powerless to make things happen. It is especially
difficult to bear such waiting if you think that it is God who has
brought you to this place of darkness.

What makes such waiting bearable is the belief that it is part of
our response to God to stay with it, and that our journey thus far
has led us to this point. It helps to believe that God is at work in
the depths, if not at the level of the senses, and that God is coming.

GOD IS COMING

'Grace to you and peace from him who is and who was and who is
to come'. (Revelation 1.4.) One might expect 'who is and who was
and who will be' instead of 'who is and who was and who is to
come'.[27] It's a verse that encapsulates the Biblical understanding that
our God is a God who is always coming, and his coming can impress
upon our present.

Our experience of waiting in the darkness becomes a consecrated
waiting and a darkness expectant of the dawn. Dag Hammarskjold
captures this longing expectancy when he writes:

'I am being driven forward
Into an unknown land,
The pass grows steeper,
The air colder and sharper,
A wind from my unknown goal
Stirs the strings of expectation.

Still the question:
Shall I ever get there?
There where life resounds,
A clear pure note in the silence.[28]

'A wind from my unknown goal stirs the strings of expectation.'
When the future throws its shadows on the present, when we hear
the distant sound of God's coming, when the wind of the Spirit
wafts over us then the waiting becomes full of hope. It is like
children waiting for Christmas who know that presents have been
bought and hidden – there is a certainty and yet an unknowing.[29]

Above all we discover that the timing is out of our hands to a large extent. Despite outer circumstances the waiting is full of hope. The silence of God is full of loving communication which sustains us in the depth of our being even when we cannot sustain ourselves, and our sense of non-existence is held by a deeply embedded sense of Being. Etty Hillesum describes this in a concentration camp during the Second World War:

> I got a letter from Leguit that touched me very much ... He enclosed a quotation from Dr. Korff: 'And yet God is love'. I completely agree, and it is truer now than ever ... I have noticed that in every situation, even the most difficult, man generates new faculties that help him keep on living. As far as that is concerned, God is merciful enough ... 'The realms of the soul and the spirit are so spacious and unending ... I do not feel I have been robbed of my freedom, essentially no one can do me any harm at all'.
>
> The misery here is quite terrible; and yet, late at night when the day has slunk away into the depths behind me, I often walk with a spring in my step beside the barbed wire. And then time and again it soars from my heart – I can't help it, that's just the way it is, like some elementary force – the feeling that life is glorious and magnificent ... We may suffer, but we must not succumb.[30]

BREAKING DOWN AND BREAKING IN

The meaning and weight we give to an event changes not only our perception but our ability to live through it, particularly if it is traumatic. When life seems to be breaking down, such times of impasse are described vividly by Constance Fitzgerald:

> By impasse I mean that there is no way out of, no way around, no rational escape from, what imprisons one, no possibilities in the situation. In a true impasse, every normal manner of acting is brought to a standstill, and ironically, impasse is experienced not only in the problem itself but also in any solution rationally attempted. Every logical solution remains unsatisfying, at the very least ... Any movement out, any next step, is cancelled, and the most dangerous temptation is to give up, to quit, to surrender to cynicism and despair, in the face of the disappointment, disenchantment, hopelessness, and loss of meaning that encompasses one.[31]

In such a situation it is no good being told that 'time heals'. All time does is pass slowly. Healing is something else. The original quotation from Hippocrates (460–357 BCE) tells us that 'Healing is a matter of time, but it is also sometimes a matter of opportunity.'[32] Growing through an impasse is not a matter of passively waiting for time to pass and healing to happen. It is about taking opportunities to promote healing and nurture growth. Such opportunities are a gift and also a result of our seeking.

Whilst we may be experiencing a sense of life *breaking down*, God may be trying to *break in*. Though God hides himself (Isaiah 45: 15), this silent and hidden God is not absent but present in the darkness. God is trying to break in.

Time passes – what the New Testament calls 'chronos'. The scriptures mention another kind of time – '*kairos*'. *Kairos* is a time of disjunction when God is breaking in, in a new way. *Kairos* time therefore gives an element of hope that chronos time can never give. In *kairos* time God is seeking to make himself known in a decisive way. Mary Craig writes of such a time in her own life when she is caring for her second child, Paul, who was born with gargoylism:

> . . . I had come to the end of the road in more ways than one. I had lost sight of myself as a person, I viewed the future with fear, and I realised with a shock that even my rather vague religion had deserted me. I no longer believed in God . . . the whole idea of a loving God was a hollow sham, a cosmic joke . . . But there was no way out of the impasse and I could only go on compounding the meaninglessness. Suicide . . . would only have shifted the whole ghastly mess into someone else's court . . . somehow that same evening I found myself alone in a church. I muttered a defiant . . . 'Damn you, you don't exist, but I hate you'. Then I threw decorum to the winds, 'if you do exist show me a way out. For a start what am I to do next?'[33]

She found herself drawn to work at the Sue Ryder Home at Cavendish in Suffolk for survivors of Nazi concentration camps:

> . . . As long as I live, I will never be able to forget that first visit to Cavendish. . . . In fact I was being shaken up and turned inside out . . . I had gone to Cavendish to get away from my own troubles . . . looking for a place to hide . . .[34]
>
> . . . The survivors showed me another possibility: that one could live with pain precisely by not fighting it; by not denying its existence . . . using it, going beyond it . . .[35]

At these times of impasse, when we are most broken and vulnerable, God may break through in the most unexpected and maybe painful of ways. In the ensuing silence we may become aware of the presence we had long ignored.

SILENCE FOR GOD

There are no words,
they hang, like ill-fitting coats,
upon an awe
which only speaks
in SILENCE
There are no words
Only a Word,
a presence,
which blows in by His
choosing
and scatters graces
eagerly upon us.
There are no words.
Instead, the music of eternity
played out in
silent love,
and we are lost in Him

These words were written after the meeting of a group of people who had deeply shared their life stories. Gradually a silence descended on the group as the truth of each person was honoured and respected. Into their truth came a sense of presence – another truth, which was building relationships of love and trust. Sometimes such silence comes upon us. At other times we make time for silence with God.

These may be regular slots in our day or week, the silence offered by going away on retreat or just going for a walk. In fact these less formal times are often when we lower our masks and barriers and become aware of another who is with us. This is God's 'unobtrusive silence', 'communicative silence' – a silence simply to be enjoyed – a sign of God's longing for us, a reminder that he is on the inside of our longing for life and for him.

All your love, your stretching out, your hope, your thirst, God is creating in you so that he may fill you. It is not your desire that makes it happen, but his. He longs through your heart. Your insufficiency and your forgetting to long for him are no barrier. In your prayer God is seeking you and himself creating the prayer: He is on the inside of your longing.[36]

SUFFERING AND SILENCE

In this chapter we have looked at the power of silence and the need to feel it whether it is destructive or a painful but necessary part of our growth. We have highlighted the difference between loneliness and all-one-ness, and have explored God's silence.

SUFFERING AND CREATIVITY

I got a Micro-processor,
My mother hangs around,
She forgets that I can operate
Without her efforts now.
Nobody can imagine,
My escape route from despair,
It came from many nations,
Who read *The Times* as
Sunday prayer. The surplus
Money may provide many mighty
Mesmerising dreams, for
Handicapped – imprisoned, isolated
Tongue-tied, to feel welcomed
By the world – released.[1]

Christopher Nolan was eleven years old before anyone knew he could write. This poem was written when he was fourteen and reflecting on his first computer, which he described as 'my escape route from despair'. The ability to communicate and be creative is often precisely that. In this chapter we look at creative responses to suffering.

CONNECTION AND DISTINCTION

We have touched on the question of connecting with those who suffer while remaining distinct from them. In this chapter we explore this further in terms of our own suffering and that of others. At one level, it comes down to a question of identity. When we are in affliction our suffering is total. We *are* suffering . . . we are abuse. The pain is total. All we can do is survive, to endure, or to succumb and the choice may not be ours. As soon as we can get any distance at all from our suffering so that it is not a question of being total pain but being a person in pain we can begin to make choices. We are connected to our suffering but also distinct from it. Our identity involves our suffering but is not subsumed by it.

It took Jackie and I some time to make this discovery. Her disease was pulling us apart. She was engulfed by it and my whole life was dominated by it. We would take out our anger and frustration on each other. When we identified the disease as a third party we were both grappling with, we found a deeper sense of connectedness with each other. Together we had to work against the effects of this disease to continue living fully in whatever ways we could.

The ability to become distinct from the disease, as a couple, enabled us to cope better with what was happening. It is important to keep sight of our humanity – for example, not to talk of the 'MS sufferer' but of Jane who has MS. We need to be careful not to define people by only one aspect of their identity, nor to define ourselves that way.

James L Empereuer makes a similar point when he says that it is easy for those coming to terms with being gay to forsake their former identity and take on the 'identity' of the gay sub-culture,[3] as though being gay was the principal and defining aspect of their personality. In truth, when one aspect has brought suffering, rejection, and alienation it is not unusual for the pendulum to swing the other way. People coming to terms with their 'rejected selves' may then seek to forge their own identity and become 'inter-individual people' – that is, 'people who are free enough to be themselves and let others be themselves fully'.[4]

This is the goal for all who seek maturity even if the only maturity we achieve is to recognise our immaturity.[5] To achieve even this self-insight requires a quality of reflection that allows us to be distant as well as being fully connected with our true selves. As Dag Hammarskjold points out, so often the need to belong stems from our fears and needs to be seen for what it is:

> Don't be afraid of yourself – live your individuality to the full – but for the good of others. Don't copy others in order to buy fellowship . . .[6]

For the Christian our identity is primarily that which is 'hid with Christ in God'. In recognising our identity there we are both connected with the facts of our existence but also set free from being totally constrained by them, even when they contain our pain.[7] In accepting both our connectedness and distinctiveness from others we not only preserve our own unique humanity but also respect the unique humanity of others.

HUMANITY

In chapter 3 we emphasised the importance of preserving a respect for humanity. This respect for humanity gives us the opportunity to be creative in response to suffering. It means not allowing ourselves to demonise others. Desmond Tutu, Brian Keenan[8] and Kathleen Fischer[9] all make this fundamental point. Desmond Tutu writes:

> Malusi Mpumlwana, now a priest . . . was in the late 1970s and early 1980s a young enthusiastic activist . . . He said that in his frequent stints in detention the security police had told him, 'We are running this country,' and when they routinely tortured him he used to think, 'These are God's children and yet they are behaving like animals. They need us to help them recover the humanity they have lost.'[10]

This has implications not only for ourselves but for all who offer any kind of support or therapy – and for the role of religion itself. Schillebeeckz writes:

> A religion which in fact has a dehumanising effect, in whatever way, is either a false religion or a religion which understands itself wrongly.[11]

SUFFERING AND CREATIVITY

There is then in suffering the opportunity to be creative, to recognise our connection with and also our distinctiveness from the suffering we face. We can do this by being creative not only within the situation but outside it – by expressing our most intimate selves in words, music, art or drama, for example. It is to this that we now turn.

> We must keep the patient busy,
> We must get the patient moving,
> There must never be a moment when the patient's lying still –
> We must boost the patient's ego
> With macramé or with Lego –
> If we leave him for a minute he will think that he is ill.
>
> We must stop him being lazy,

We must drive the patient crazy.
Give him crosswords, give him Scrabble, and manipulate his
    knee.
We will let him win at Cluedo,
Then tomorrow try some judo,
He'll be beating Peter Elliott within a week, you'll see.[12]

Of course there are different kinds of creativity The kind of creativity that allows us to connect with ourselves but not be bound by the facts of our condition has two possibilities – it either lets us transcend our limitations or it lets us be more fully who we are within our limitations. Creativity may be either active or passive depending upon how we see things. Either way is growth – outward or inward.

BEAUTY

When a friend heard that I was going to write a book about suffering she remembered her college days and a dissertation about suffering that had almost brought her to despair. What saved her was taking a break from it and refreshing herself with long walks, music, and art. Somehow an eye and ear for beauty put some balance back into her life.[13] It may seem simplistic to suggest that beauty can have any meaning at all in the face of abject suffering. Indeed it cannot be overstressed that we are talking about suffering which allows some distance to be gained in order to be able to make a response other than just endurance. The joy of beauty is that it prevents us giving suffering the ultimate power over us which allows it to define who we are and how the world is. To give suffering such power is to deny our own humanity. It is said of Etty Hillesum that:

> She refused to deny the presence and importance of beauty even in the midst of the pain and brokenness of an occupied country . . . There is a sense in which pessimism can become a self-fulfilling prophecy: we expect to see evil and therefore we fail to look for the good and the beautiful . . . she disarms evil not by denying its existence – that would be naive and foolish – but by denying its power ultimately to define what life is all about.[14]

In the ability to be touched by beauty even in suffering we discover the ability to transcend ourselves in the sight of a glorious view, a piece of jasmine outside a concentration camp window[15], a bowl of oranges[16], or a single rose against the background of experiencing the First World War:

> There is a world of wonder in this rose;
> God made it, and his whole creation grows
> To a point of perfect beauty
> In this garden plot. He knows
> The poet's thrill
> On this June morning, as He sees
> His Will
> To beauty taking form, His word
> Made flesh, and dwelling among men.
> All mysteries
> In this one flower meet
> And intertwine,
> The universal is concrete
> The human and divine,
> In one unique and perfect thing, are fused
> Into a unity of Love,
> This rose as I behold it;
> For all things gave it me,
> The stars have helped to mould it,
> The air, soft moonshine, and the rain,
> The meekness of old mother earth,
> The many-billowed sea.
> The evolution of ten million years,
> And all the pain
> Of ages, brought it to its birth
> And gave it me.
> The tears
> Of Christ are in it,
> And His Blood
> Has dyed it red,
> I could not see it but for Him
> Because He led
> Me to the Love of God,
> From, which all Beauty springs
> I and my rose
> Are one.[17]

Beauty may be seen in nature or in the creative work of others or of ourselves. It may be the beauty of music, of art, of another's face and hands, and touch:

> ... for Christ plays in ten thousand places,
>   Lovely in limbs, and lovely in eyes not his
>   To the Father through the features of men's faces.[18]

To gaze at what is beautiful and to long for the beloved is the means of our transformation and growth. Beauty and love go together. We may gaze at what is attractive to the eye, contemplate its beauty, and find ourselves touched somehow by the mystery of the beloved. Paradoxically, we may also find that in being touched by the beloved, touched by love, we may gaze at that which is not obviously beautiful and discover a hidden beauty even in apparent ugliness. In other words we may give beauty to another by looking with love. So it is that we are caught up in divine loving – even when we are incapable of doing anything else. For St Augustine, beauty expressed the utter loveliness and desirability of the one whom he was seeking. He draws us to look at Christ himself, whose beauty 'compels beyond all other, beyond ten thousand rivals'.[19]

CREATIVE RESPONSE

How may we respond creatively in the face of suffering? So much depends not only on what is happening to us but on the way we respond, and how others alongside us may enable us to respond.

Jackie was an artist. She painted and sketched and also used fabrics and threads to create beauty. Her disease inflicted a creeping disability. She could no longer care for her children in a physical way, nor paint, nor use her sewing machine unaided. Friends came to help her. Two friends came in regularly, got out her painting equipment for her and devised inventive ways of enabling her to paint so that she was still painting two weeks before she died. Another friend who was very able with a needle translated Jackie's ideas into the clothes that she needed to make being in a wheelchair easier. Through the help of others she was still creative and through her desire to create they were creative too in ways that might otherwise not have been.

What makes it possible to make a creative response is, perhaps, recognising that it is possible to be flexible. We accept the new situation not as a victim but as master by being able to be oneself in a different way and not allowing it to define the limits of our existence but rather reaching beyond it. One lady put it this way as she came to terms with the fact that she wasn't being healed in a physical sense: 'My wound was unchanged, but I was not.'[20]

Somehow when we cannot change the situation we can change our response and our perception of the situation. For one hospice patient the change was seen as the difference between being the Good Samaritan and being the wounded one who needed help. She writes:

> It is hard: it would be unbearable were it not for my belief that the wounded man and the Samaritan are inseparable. It was the helplessness of the one that brought out the best in the other and linked them together.[21]

There are two aspects of this response that require attention - acceptance of the changed situation and acceptance that allowing others to help may actually enrich them as well as us. Acceptance is never easy no matter how much psychotherapists and spiritual directors tell us the facts are friendly.[22] Etty Hillesum speaks with a different kind of authority, however:

> The human suffering that we have seen during the last six months, and still see daily, is more than anyone can be expected to comprehend in half a year. No wonder we hear on all sides every day, in every pitch of voice, 'We don't want to think, we don't want to feel, we want to forget as soon as possible.' It seems to me that this is a very great danger . . . if we abandon the heard facts that we are forced to face, if we give them no shelter in our heads and hearts, do not allow them to settle and change into impulses through which we can grow and from which we can draw meaning . . . if we fail to draw new meaning from the deep wells of our distress, then it will not be enough.[23]

Accepting the changed situation is to bear an enormous cost and takes time and energy if it is to be achieved as we face the anger, denial and yearning that echoes our grief. But should we come to acceptance we might be more ready to receive help and help itself may help us reach acceptance.

A friend of mine is a music therapist. One day she showed me a recording of a session with a patient.

I found myself in tears. The therapist sat at a piano with a man who had had a severe stroke and who could not normally communicate. At first he played random notes whilst she improvised an accompaniment. There was little connection between the two. Gradually he began to listen to her as she listened to him and some melodies emerged. There was communication. And then she sang and invited him to sing. Singing did not come naturally to him but as he relaxed he began to sing. Centred in himself, the man was able to communicate through the singing. He even teased the therapist and he laughed and she laughed with him. There was so much beauty and fun in their song, it had a transcendent grace as he was lifted out of himself into this dialogue of love. Yet paradoxically he was taken more deeply into his inner being – the self not touched by the stroke. His soul was singing. To listen to their song was to have one's own soul touched. No wonder there were tears.[24]

This is a good example of Edwin Muir's sense of the annunciation, 'I sing the liberty/Where each asks from each/What each most wants to give/And each awakes in each/What else would never be.'[25]

There is in such 'being alongside' a connection and a distinction which gives rise to something greater than either could do or be on their own. It is almost as though the music finds the participants. That is not to deny the musical competence of the therapist but it affirms that the therapist and the client must listen to each other through the music as well as through visual contact for the beauty and the communication to emerge.

If artistic endeavour is to help us through suffering, there are a number of elements involved: connection and distinction, self-expression tempered by listening to the 'other' whether this is a friend, relative, therapist, a group or society as a whole.

Being able to respond creatively is very different from 'positive thinking'. One seeks to focus on the positive, while the other goes deeper, and does not deny the negative; instead it seeks to accept and transcend it, and to keep hold of a *whole* picture of humanity.

CREATIVE ENDEAVOUR

Then mother managed to buy me some more paints and brushes, along with one or two drawing books and a pencil. This, of course, broadened my range of expression and allowed me to have a greater choice of subject. After the first few weeks of uncertainty and awkwardness, I settled down contentedly with my new pastime. I painted every day upstairs in the back bedroom, completely by myself.

I was changing. I didn't know it then, but I had found a way to be happy again and to forget some of the things that had made me unhappy. Above all I learned to forget myself. I didn't miss going out with my brothers now, for I had something to keep my mind active, something to make each day a thing to look forward to.

I would sit crouched on the floor for hours, holding the brush between my toes, my right leg curled up under my left, my arms held tightly at my sides, the hands clenched. All my paints and brushes were around me, and I would get my mother or father to pin the drawing paper to the floor with tacks to keep it steady. It looked a very awkward position, with my head almost between my knees and my back as crooked as a cork-screw. But I painted all my best pictures in this way, with the wooden floor as my easel.

Slowly I began to lose my early depression. I had a feeling of pure joy while I painted, a feeling I had never experienced before and which seemed almost to lift me above myself. It was only when I wasn't painting that I became depressed and cross with everyone at home.[26]

Christy Brown reveals the importance of finding a means of self-expression but self-expression, though cathartic, is not the same as communicating and relating. Later Christy was to write stories and books.

A music therapist, Gary Ansdell, emphasises both these aspects of creativity and of creative therapy:

(the arts) . . . create order and meaning in the face of disorder and meaninglessness . . .[27]

He [Maslow] investigated both the necessary conditions and strategies people used to keep themselves healthy and happy. Being and staying creative he found to be one of the most important of these.[28]

art therapies . . . work with what is integral to a person, not just their handicap or illness . . .[29]

We also need to keep in mind the notion of the arts as a *challenge to set ways of feeling, thinking or acting.*[30]

These last two emphasise the need for the therapist to connect with the patient at the level of humanity and also to be able through the music to express that connection and the distinctiveness that may enable the patient to 'experience themselves in a new way'.[31]

There is then a centering – a connection with self and a standing apart from oneself – a distinction or seeing oneself differently. This enables the self to reach beyond the present situation with a change of perspective which is made possible by the presence and competence of a therapist. We shall explore this 'centering' and 'reaching beyond' later in the chapter.

In this creative endeavour there is the possibility of a new freedom not only of expression but of relating, setting free to live in the present moment. It may be that despite the agony and pain endured, the person who has suffered may find a deeper level of being and meaning than they had previously experienced.

> That is the God-content of pain: it has the power to unlock us at the point where we cannot unlock ourselves . . . healing comes particularly in situations that take us out of our own control.[33]

Here Iain Matthew is talking of John's 'Night'. We see John of the Cross's awareness of how the past and the future can paralyse us and how experiencing the night can free us:

> John is himself masterfully aware . . . of how the roots from the past can tyrannise the emotions; and of how the future can paralyse with worry one's fluidity in the here and now.[34]

Put simply, whatever absorbs us and is outside ourselves can enable us to be fluid in the here and now. The arts have an invaluable contribution to make because they portray a different reality from our own and enable us to see ourselves and life differently. They can enable us to deal with our sense of disintegration, find a different orientation to life and an integration that rises above mere conformity. We are reminded of Stanley Spencer's comment about the painting of the chapel at Burghclere: 'The Burghclere memorial redeemed my experience from what it was; namely something alien to me. By this means I recover my lost self'. Other examples could be drawn from all the arts and from the use of art and music in formal and informal therapy.

CENTERING AND REACHING BEYOND

> Disintegration, disorder, disconnection – these have always been descriptions of illness, whilst their opposites – integration, order and connection – are, as Oliver Sacks has remarked, the necessary qualities of any therapy. 'One way of "centring", of

recalling a self, the active powers of a self, from the abyss of pathology, can be given by music, by art of all kinds.[35]

In the example of the music therapy session with a stroke victim it is clear that music has the power to centre a person and enable them to reach beyond the limitations that illness has imposed upon them. This power may be transitory and when the therapy is over the person will obviously have been affected by, it but may be able to reach that level of deep communication only in the context of music. This is not to undermine the value of the therapy but to clarify what is true for all of us. The experience of being totally centred and able to feel connected with life and everything in it so as to reach beyond ourselves is transitory for most of us. When it happens, it is a catalyst in our transformation. One way of using suffering is to accept that suffering itself may be a tool of transcendence as well as of limitation. This is the gift of freedom within ourselves that Brian Keenan enjoyed even in captivity.

There are two ways of experiencing freedom and two ways of personal growth – linear and spiral. Linear growth can be seen to be progressive and is often measured by achievements. Personal growth may be more of a spiral process. We grow more deeply into ourselves by apparently learning the same lesson often but in reality meeting similar circumstances at a deeper level – we're on the same point of a circle but at a different turn of the spiral.

Becoming centred means that we are content to live with our ability to go down (and up) the spiral, accepting our different perceptions as part of a greater whole. Being able to reach beyond ourselves means being able to move beyond our present circumstances (not being constrained by them). It also means being able, within our present circumstances, to find a different experience of ourself. The first will look to others like linear growth. They may see some improvement in our condition. The second will be perceived less in those terms but may mean that we have become more accepting of ourself, and more centred.

THE BELOVED

Music and art may help people reach beyond themselves by becoming absorbed in 'that which is other'. Etty Hillesum, in the camp at Westerbork, finds herself absorbed not only by suffering, humanity and beauty but by God. Here in her Beloved she discovers her own centre and her ability to reach beyond herself.

You have made me so rich, oh God, please let me share out Your beauty with open hands. My life has become an uninterrupted dialogue with You, oh God, one great dialogue . . . Things come and go in a deeper rhythm, and people must be taught to listen; it is the most important thing we have to learn in this life . . . Sometimes I try my hand at turning out small profundities and uncertain short stories, but I always end up with just one single word: God. And that says everything, and there is no need for anything more . . . The beat of my heart has grown deeper, more active, and yet more peaceful, and it is as if all the time I were storing up inner riches.[36]

In the darkness and isolation of his prison, John of the Cross makes a similar discovery that the Beloved is all.

The joy of knowing the Beloved is not that the Beloved saves us from suffering but that he connects with our humanity and so with our suffering. He is not the same as us but distinct from us. This attitude to suffering of connection and distinction is, in the end, nothing more or less than an attitude of love. Quite simply if we are to use our own suffering or alleviate the suffering of another our starting place is love.

LOVE

'Love has a paschal rhythm', or as Etty Hillesum says, 'Things come and go in a deeper rhythm'. This reminds us that life involves painful change as well as great beauty and joy.

It's well summarised by the Taizé Rule for a new brother:

Your way through life
Will not remain the same.
There are years of happiness and years of suffering.
There are years of abundance,
and years of poverty,
years of hope, and of disappointment,
of building up, and of breaking down.
But God has a firm hold on you through everything
There are years of strength
and years of weakness,
years of uncertainty, years of doubt.
It is all part of life,
and it is worth the effort

to live it to the end
and not give up before it is
accomplished.

You need never stop growing
A new future is always possible.
Even on the other side of death
a new existence waits for you
in the fulness of that glory
which God has prepared for you
from the beginning.[37]

How are we to use suffering? Simply by choosing life, even in
the midst of suffering. A man suffering from motor neurone disease,
forced to lie all day on his side in bed, communicating only by
computer and with a straw in his mouth, puts it this way:

> it has been 4 years since i could hold a pen . . . i was angry for
> about three years. it ate me up. Then I stopped being angry.
> now I pray to jesus christ . . . feel that I have to choose to live
> even now which is hard for someone so tired . . . better to know
> and grow from the experience than to remain aloof and have
> no basis for wisdom . . .[38]

Such an attitude is powerful in its acceptance and reality, in its
love and trust. It conveys a willingness to let suffering be a teacher.
It is the option for life.

THE OPTION FOR LIFE

On this note this chapter and this book comes to an end. The
question is whether we choose life not only at the point when
suffering confronts us but in those times of the paschal rhythm –
the rhythm of growth, decay and new life, when things are going
well. In chapter 2 we raised the issue of coming to an awareness of
our moral identity at such times. In chapter 3 the need to embrace
and love into healing, our shadow and darkness, at such times. In
chapter 5 the need to question the individualism that lies at the
heart of much of life, which is fine when life is going well but which
leaves us totally isolated when life is going through the doldrums.
In terms of faith we have suggested that the ability to trust without
strings is often the way in which we find ourselves engaged not
only with suffering but with the God content of pain. That trust

without strings is developed by getting to know God for ourselves, whether through conventional religion or not. The scriptures, and especially the psalms, seem to be unique in coming to people's aid when the darkness is around them. As we said of Jesus, 'The psalm that entered his soul through prayer now speaks from his soul in desperation'. In our good times we have the opportunity to fill our inner store cupboard with resources for the lean times – spiritual, aesthetic, sacramental and through prayer and silence. What the scriptures offer us above all is an awareness of the paschal rhythm of love revealed in a human being.

There is a challenge here that we easily recognise in terms of health, finance or housekeeping but fail to recognise in the life of the spirit. It is simply that withstanding difficult times relates very much to the reality with which we have addressed our spiritual life in the good times. The time to be concerned about the truth of our lives is now.

Life demanded that the book be finished. Other work had to take precedence. In a few weeks' time he was to move house and take up some challenging work, and anyway, he had nothing else to say.

He went, alone, to pray. He pondered suffering and this man Jesus who had sometimes been elusive, often hidden by associations that had not been helpful – a Jesus whom he had learnt to trust again and know afresh five years after the trauma of his wife dying – Jesus who knew about suffering – who had been there, done that and got the tee-shirt.

He gazed at him, looked at the tee-shirt. The words on the tee-shirt seemed faded. Too much blood had been soaked into it, it had been washed so many times. It had seen so many others through their suffering. As he gazed, so the words became clearer. Emblazoned on the shirt that covered the wounded side were the words 'Trust without strings' and beneath them a single word – Love.

NOTES

INTRODUCTION
1. George Appleton, *In His Name* (London, Macmillan, 1956), p. 60.
2. Wilfrid Owen, *The Poems* (London, Chatto & Windus, 1969), p. 40.
3. Christopher Nolan, *Dam-burst of Dreams* (London, Sphere, 1982), p. 39.

CHAPTER 1: SUFFERING IN OUR LIFE
1. W.H.Auden, *Collected Poems* (London, Faber & Faber, 1976), p. 179.
2. Osip Mandelshtam, *Selected Poems* trans. with notes by James Greene (London, Penguin, 1991), p. 49.
3. Hans Kung, *On Being a Christian* (Glasgow, Fount, 1978), p. 576. In a masterly description of our response to suffering Kung suggests that we should not seek but bear suffering; that we should not only bear suffering but fight it; that we should not only fight suffering but use it to find freedom.
4. Ivan Mann (ed.), *The Golden Key* (Northampton, Motor Neurone Disease Association, 1990), p. 80.
5. The case for this is well stated in Donald Nicholl, *The Beatitude of Truth* (London, DLT, 1997), ch. 4.
6. Brian Keenan, *An Evil Cradling* (London, Hutchinson, 1992), p. 250.
7. Brian Keenan and John McCarthy, *Between Extremes* (London, Bantam, 1999), p. 82.
8. James A. Whyte, *Laughter and Tears* (Edinburgh, St. Andrew Press, 1993), p. 95.
9. This phrase has been in my mind for twenty years and is the genesis of this book. George Appleton, *In His Name* (London, Macmillan, 1957), p. 62.
10. '... when you think of the mystical experience of many saints, you may ask yourself whether joy and suffering aren't aspects of the same phenomenon at a very high level. An analogy, crazy for sure, comes to my mind: extreme cold burns. It seems nearly certain, no, it is certain that we can only go to God through suffering and that this suffering becomes joy because it finally is the same thing.' *Une Grande Amitie: Correspondence 1926–1972 Julien Green – Jacques Maritain* (Paris, Gallimard, 1982), quoted in Henri J. M. Nouwen, *Life of the Beloved* (London, Hodder & Stoughton, 1992), p. 108.
11. Rowan Williams, *Open to Judgement* (London, DLT, 1998), p. 55.
12. 'From Christ's dread and humiliation flows the grace that can work in all dread and humiliation. It does not demand from us passivity, resignation, but the acceptance that will turn us in a new enlightened understanding to the crooked heart of our neighbour; so that my memory of privation and hurt itself becomes part of what I can offer, in intelligent compassion, to the hurts of others. That is sanctity: the wholeness of giving the gift of all your self.' ibid. p. 211f.
13. *Stanley Spencer at Burghclere* (London, The National Trust, 1991) p. 10.
14. Kenneth Pople, *Stanley Spencer* (London, Collins, 1991), p. 110.
15. ibid. p. 132.
16. ibid. p. 128.
17. ibid. p. 136.
18. ibid. p. 158.
19. ibid. p. 165.
20. ibid. p. 257.

CHAPTER 2: ALLEVIATING SUFFERING

1. Dietrich Bonhoeffer, *Letters and Papers from Prison* (Enlarged Edition) (London, SCM, 1971), p. 334.
2. Gerard Manley Hopkins, *The Poems of Gerard Manley Hopkins* (London, OUP, 1949), p. 106.
3. Martin Israel, *Dark Victory* (London, Mowbray, 1995), p. 93.
4. Jonathan Glover, *Humanity* (London, Jonathan Cape, 1999) – to which I am greatly indebted in this chapter.
5. ibid. p. 35.
6. ibid. p. 89.
7. ibid. p. 26. The term 'moral identity is described by Jonathan Glover thus: 'this sense of identity has a moral charge when it is not a matter of style or personality but is of deeper character. A person's character . . . comes partly from individual decisions and actions. Repeated, these become the habits that set into character. The ways that we respond to things that happen and to things people do also play a part. These responses may have no reference to ourselves. We may respect loyalty or detest cruelty when we see them in others. They leave a residue of personal commitment, perhaps to being a loyal friend, a good Catholic, being someone who would not work for a tobacco company, or being someone to speak out in an unpopular cause, few people could easily give a list of what their own commitments are. We may only recognise them when we are challenged. But these commitments, even if hardly conscious, are the core of moral identity.'
8. ibid. pp. 22–5. Among human responses, respect and sympathy for others are key.
9. ibid. p. 28.
10. Cicely Saunders, *Hospice and Palliative Care: An Interdisciplinary Approach* (London, Edward Arnold, 1990), p. 27.
11. Simone Weil, *Waiting for God* (London, Fountain, 1977), pp. 76ff. 'In the realm of suffering affliction is something apart, specific and irreducible. It is quite a different thing from simple suffering. It takes possession of the soul and marks it through and through with its own particular mark, the mark of slavery. . .

    'Affliction is an uprooting of life, a more or less attenuated equivalent of death, made irresistibly present to the soul by the attack or immediate apprehension of physical pain. . . we count as physical pain certain phenomena which, though difficult to describe, are bodily and exactly equivalent to it. Fear of physical pain is a notable example. . .

    'There is not real affliction unless the event which has seized and uprooted a life attacks it directly or indirectly, in all its parts, *social, psychological* and *physical*. The social factor is essential. There is not really affliction where there is not social degradation or the fear of it in some form or another.'
12. Cicely Saunders, *Hospice and Palliative Care*, p. 14.
13. This could be the theme of another book on the need to find a balance between care provided by society, by family and by the charities. All have a responsibility towards those who suffer. None can bear that responsibility alone. Familial help includes friends who are for many the immediately available 'family'.
14. Susan S. Lang and Richard B. Patt MD, *You Don't Have to Suffer* (Oxford, OUP, 1994), p. 275.
15. Keenan, *An Evil Cradling*, p 31.
16. Elisabeth Kubler-Ross, *On Death and Dying* (London, Tavistock, 1979), p. 35.
17. Deric Longden, *Diana's Story* (London, Bantam, 1989), p. 59.
18. Dorothee Soelle, *Suffering* (London, DLT, 1972), p. 11.
19. Edmund Blunden (ed.), *The Poems of Wilfrid Owen* (London, Chatto & Windus, 1969), p. 117.
20. Jonathan Glover, *Humanity* p. 409.
21. Vanessa Herrick and Ivan Mann, *Jesus Wept* (London, DLT, 1998),p. 162.
22. Keenan, p. 217.
23. Sheila Cassidy, *Sharing the Darkness* (London, DLT, 1988), p. 55.

24. Keenan, p. 230.
25. 'The Healing', Virginia Thesiger in Elizabeth Basset (ed.) *Love Is My Meaning* (London, DLT, 1986), p. 143.
26. Donald Nicholl, *The Beatitude of Truth* (London, DLT, 1999).
27. Quoted in *The Journal of Health Care Chaplaincy* (The College of Health Care Chaplains, February 2000, Vol 3: No 2), p. 4.

CHAPTER 3: SUFFERING IN OURSELVES

1. Gerard Manley Hopkins, *Poems of Gerard Manley Hopkins* (London, Oxford University Press, 1949), p. 95.
2. John Macquarrie, *Principles of Christian Theology* (London, SCM, 1975), p. 56.
3. quoted in Norman White, *Hopkins* (Oxford, Clarendon Press, 1992), p. 443.
4. ibid. p. 440.
5. *Poems of Gerard Manley Hopkins*, p. 112.
6. Robert Bernard Martin, *Gerard Manley Hopkins: A very private life* (London, Flamingo, 1992), p. 413.
7. ibid. p. 415
8. ibid. p. 263
9. In our own day perhaps Sylvia Plath is the best-known poet who wrote out of the crucible of her own pain.
10. John Macquarrie, p. 56.
11. Using Simone Weil's definition of affliction may help us to see some positive ways of alleviating suffering. We might want to add a fourth – suffering of the Spirit which may embrace all three and at its worst may be experienced as total pain.
12. Diana Dewar, *Saint of Auschwitz* (London, DLT, 1982), p. 108.
13. D. H., Lawrence, 'Shadows', *D.H.Lawrence: The Complete Poems* (Harmondsworth, Penguin, 1980), p. 726. See also 'The Phoenix' p. 728.
14. Edmund Blunden (ed.), *The Poems of Wilfrid Owen* (London, Chatto & Windus, 1969), p. 40.
15. Pat Barker, *Regeneration* (London, Penguin, 1991), p. 3.
16. 'Dreamers' by Siegfried Sassoon in Robert Giddings, *The War Poets* (London, Bloomsbury, 1988), p. 143.
17. ibid. p. 108.
18. ibid. p. 107.
19. Susan Hill, *Strange Meeting* (London, Penguin, 1989) p. 180. In chapter 2 we saw how the painting of the Chapel at Burghclere 'redeemed' the experience of the First World War for Spencer. Susan Hill writes about her own fascination with the subject 'I was haunted by it for years and in writing the novel I laid the ghost forever . . .'
20. See also Brian Keenan and John McCarthy, *Between Extremes*, on a similar theme.
21. Susan Hill, *Strange Meeting*, p. 12.
22. ibid. p. 178.
23. Keenan, *An Evil Cradling* p. 112.
24. ibid. p. 287.
25. See, e.g, Michael Korda, *Man to Man* (London, Little Brown, 1997), p 223f.
26. Alan Coren, from the Alternative Version, further source unknown.
27. 'Disfigured by sin and death, man remains "in the image of God", in the image of the Son, but is deprived "of the glory of God", of his "likeness". The promise made to Abraham inaugurates the economy of salvation, at the culmination of which the Son will assume that "image" and restore it to the Father's "likeness" by giving it again its Glory, the Spirit who is "the giver of life." ' *Catechism of the Catholic Church* (London, Geoffrey Chapman, 1994), para. 705.
28. See e.g. Carl Rogers, *On Becoming a Person* (London, Constable, 1997).
29. Sojourner Truth quoted in Julia Neuberger, *The Things That Matter* (London, Kyle Cathie, 1992), p. 18f.
30. It is not the intention of this book to look deeply at the psychological under-

standing of the 'shadow' though the work of Jung and of the Myers-Briggs Indicator underlies some of the understanding expressed in this chapter. Isabel Myers Briggs with Peter B. Myers, *Gifts Differing* (California, Davis-Black, 1995), p. 84f explains the shadow thus: ' . . . everyone has a *shadow side*. Just as the conscious personality is the product of the best-developed processes, the *shadow* is the product of the least developed part, which a person rejects and disowns.'

31. Jean Vanier, *Community and Growth* (London, DLT, 1989), pp. 42, 43.
32. Naomi L. Quenk, *In the Grip* (California, Consulting Psychologists Press, 1996), p. 5: 'Falling into the grip . . . is most likely to occur when a person's conscious psychic energy is at a low level . . . The following four circumstances are very effective ways in which conscious energy is diminished – Fatigue . . . Illness . . . Stress . . . Alcohol and mind altering drugs.'
33. Keenan, *An Evil Cradling*, p. 215.
34. Mother Mary Clare SLG, *Fairacres Chronicle*, Winter 1988, (Oxford, SLG Press, 1988), p. 13.
35. Keenan, *An Evil Cradling*, p. 104.
36. Dietrich Bonhoeffer, *Letters and Papers From Prison*, p. 251.
37. A Carthusian, *The Wound Of Love* (London, DLT, 1994), p. 147.

CHAPTER 4: GIVING VOICE TO SUFFERING

1. Nahum Tate, libretto for Purcell's *Dido And Aeneas*.
2. Proverbs 10: 7.
3. Dante, *Inferno* Canto 5, 1, 121.
4. Primo Levi, *The Drowned And The Saved* (London, Abacus, 1988), p. 11.
5. Yehuda Amichai in Philip Crowe, *A Whisper Will Be Heard* (London, Fount, 1994), p. xiv
6. Dorothee Soelle, *Suffering* (London, DLT, 1972), p. 68.
7. Abraham Heschel in Lucinda Vardey (ed.), *God In All Worlds* (London, Chatto & Windus, 1995), p. 336.
8. Richard L. Rubenstein and John K. Roth, *Approaches To Auschwitz* (London, SCM Press 1987), p. 179.
9. Herman Wouk, *War and Remembrance* (London, Collins, 1978), Foreword.
10. George Santayana in Desmond Tutu, *No Future Without Forgiveness* (London, Rider, 1999), p. 32.
11. Siegfried Sassoon in Robert Giddings, *The War Poets* (London, Bloomsbury, 1988), p. 181.
12. Siegfried Sassoon, *The Old Century And Seven More Years*. (London, 1938), p. 140.
13. Levi, *Collected Poems* (London, Faber & Faber, 1992), p. 64.
14. Levi, *If This Is A Man* and *The Truce* (London, Abacus, 1987), p. 15.
15. ibid.
16. Levi, *The Drowned And The Saved*, p. 15.
17. ibid p. 15. Paul Bailey, Introduction
18. ibid.
19. Levi, *Collected Poems* (London, Faber & Faber, 1992), p. 64.
20. Paul Bailey, p. xiv.
21. Elie Wiesel, *All Rivers Run To The Sea* (London, HarperCollins 1997), p. 333.
22. ibid.p. 229.
23. Soelle, p. 124
24. Soelle, p. 149.
25. In Zora Neale Hurston, *Their Eyes Were Watching God* (London, Virago, 1986), p. viii.
26. Desmond Tutu, *No Future Without Forgiveness* (London, Rider, 1999), p. 20
27. ibid. p. 3.
28. ibid. p. 12
29. Levi, *If This Is A Man* and *The Truce*, p. 32.
30. ibid. p. 57.

31. Soelle, p. 107
32. Bishop Spong in Will Leckie and Barry Stopfel, *Courage To Love* (New York, Doubleday, 1997) p. 156f.
33. ibid. p. 44.
34. ibid. p. 117
35. Marcus O'Donnell on Australian gay men, in James L. Empereur *Spiritual Direction and the Gay Person* (London, Geoffrey Chapman, 1998), p. 53.
36. Armistead Maupin, *More Tales of the City* (London, Black Swan, 1989), p. 189f.
37. Thomas Merton, *Seeds of Contemplation* (Wheathampstead, Anthony Clarke, 1994), p. 25f.
38. Francoise Susset in James L. Empereur, *Spiritual Direction and the Gay Person* (London, Geoffrey Chapman, 1998), p. 24.
39. Kathleen Fischer, *Transforming Fire* (New York, Paulist Press, 1999), p. 121.
40. Jonathan Glover, *Humanity*, p. 266.
41. The Rt Revd Richard Harries, *The Church Times*, 17 March 2000, p. 3.
42. Jonathan Glover, *Humanity*, pp. 393, 410.
43. See Jeffrey John, *'Permanent, Faithful, Stable'?* (London, DLT, 2000) especially quote on p. 51 from *The Economist*.
44. Desmond Tutu, p. 24.
45. ibid. p. 218.
46. Rowan Williams, *Open to Judgement*, p. 59.

CHAPTER 5: SUFFERING AND ISOLATION

1. Algernon Charles Swinburne, Hertha Stanzas 32 and 36 in *The Oxford Book of English Mystical Verse* (Oxford, Clarendon Press, 1917), p. 293.
2. Carl Rogers, *On Becoming a Person* (London, Constable, 1967), p. 17.
3. Dorothee Soelle, *Suffering*, p. 88.
4. ibid. p. 94.
5. For a fictional description of depression see Sebastian Faulks, *Charlotte Gray* (London, Hutchinson, 1998), p. 64.
6. Dorothee Soelle, *Suffering*, p. 10.
7. Clarissa Pinkola Estes, *Women Who Run With The Wolves* (London, Rider, 1992), p. 292.
8. Quoted in *The Way* (London, The Way Publications, April 1998), p. 154.
9. Sara Maitland, *Virgin Territory* (London, Pavane, 1986), p. 86f.
10. Rowan Williams, *Open to Judgement*, p. 51
11. Harry Blamires, *A God Who Acts* (London, SPCK, 1983), p. 49.
12. ibid. p. 22.
13. Thomas Mann, *A Death in Venice* (Harmondsworth, Penguin, 1955), p. 25.
14. Keenan, *An Evil Cradling*, p. 177. See also p. 215, 'In these conditions, there was no way to control the mind. It spun off, launched into some unholy awfulness, doubling the physical pain.'
15. Levi, *If This Is A Man*, p. 69.
16. Clarissa Pinkola Estes, p. 33.
17. Rowan Williams, p. 91.
18. Martyn Percy (ed.), *Intimate Affairs* p. 94.
19. John O'Donohue, *Anam Cara* (London, Bantam 1997), p. 48.
20. ibid. p. 41.
21. Soelle, p. 74. 'The hopelessness of certain forms of suffering – whether this is grounded in conditions that are at present petrified or whether it is unalterable – can be endured where the pain can still be articulated.'
22. Desmond Tutu, *No Future without Forgiveness* (London, Rider, 1999), p. 32.
23. See, e.g, Sheila Cassidy, *The Loneliest Journey* (London, DLT, 1995), p., 181.
24. *The Pink Paper* (London, 27 August 1999), p. 24.
25. In Peter Sweasey, *From Queer to Eternity* (London, Cassell, 1997), p. xvi.
26. Keenan, *An Evil Cradling*, p. 45.

27. ibid p. 266.
28. A phrase used originally by William Styron, borrowed from Jim Cotter, *Brainsquall* (Sheffield, Cairns Publications, 1997), p. xxi.
29. The phrase somnambulant rage comes from Brian Keenan in *An Evil Cradling* p. 68. For me, the phrase reflects the sense of being 'dead', aware of immense pain, feeling it and yet not feeling it.
30. 'You' is anyone who will just be alongside – a companion in waiting.
31. *Vulgate Version 1 Kings 19.*
32. '*Keep thy mind in hell and despair not*' Staretz Silouan in Archimandrite Sophrony *The Monk of Mount Athos* (New York, St. Vladimir's Seminary Press, 1973) 116.
33. Dietrich Bonhoeffer, *Letters and Papers from Prison*, p. 35.
34. Fyodor Dostoevsky, *The Brothers Karamazov* (Harmondsworth, Penguin, 1982), p. 381.

CHAPTER 6: CAUSING SUFFERING TO OTHERS

1. Ceri Witham, Poems by pupils of Debenham High School, Suffolk, *Dancing Words* p. 147.
2. See e.g. 1 Cor 12.
3. See David L. Fleming, *A Contemporary Reading of the Spiritual Exercises* (St Louis, IJS, 1987), p. 12. [58] '. . . . I reflect that out of me – one human person among the millions of men(sic) who live – so much evil, hatred and death can come forth. What can I compare myself to – a sewer polluting the waters of the rivers of life? a walking contagion of diseases who continues to walk throughout my world, affecting it and my fellowmen without warning?'
4. Source unknown.
5. See M. Scott Peck, *The Road Less Travelled* (London, Arrow, 1985), p. 234f. Peck suggests that many with marriage difficulties opt out of therapy rather than face the reality of divorce or the sustained and difficult work necessary in the relationship.
6. Karl Barth, *Church Dogmatics IV.1.* (Edinburgh, T & T Clark, 1956), p. 185.
7. Hans Peter Jungel, *Die gesellschaftlichen Leiden und das leiden Gesellschaft, Vorstudien zu einer Pathologie das Rollenverhaltens*, (Stuttgart, F. Enke, 1968), p. 365.
8. Soelle, p. 12.
9. See p. 62.
10. Martin Israel, *Dark Victory* (London, Mowbray, 1995), p. 45.
11. Dietrich Bonhoeffer, *Letters and Papers from Prison*, p. 14.
12. Cecil Day-Lewis, 'Walking Away'.
13. M. Scott Peck, p. 66.
14. For an exploration of this theme, see Maria Boulding, *Gateway to Hope*, (London, Fount, 1985), pp. 74 and 30.
15. ibid. p. 136.
16. Jurgen Moltmann, *The Experiment Hope* (London, SCM, 1975), p. 85.
17. Nigel Taylor, *Christian Words* (Edinburgh, T & T Clark, 1980), p. 213.
18. ibid. p. 214.
19. Ivan Mann (ed.), *The Golden Key* (Northampton, MNDA, 1990), p. 80.
20. Source unknown.

CHAPTER 7: SHARING THE SUFFERING OF OTHERS

1. Cardinal Basil Hume, in Sebastian Sandys (ed.), *Embracing the Mystery* (London, SPCK, 1992), p. 95f. Reprinted by kind permission of the copyright holders: the literary estate of the late Cardinal Basil Hume.
2. Keenan, *An Evil Cradling*. See p. 6.
3. Edmund Blunden (ed.), *The Poems of Wilfrid Owen*, (London, Chatto & Windus, 1969), p. 29.
4. Philip Caputo, *A Rumor of War*, (London, Pimlico, 1999), p. 282.
5. In her discussion of Mark 1.41 Morna Hooker, *The Gospel According to St Mark*

(London, A & C Black, 1991), p. 79f., argues that the translation 'Jesus, moved with anger' is more likely than 'Jesus, moved with pity', on the grounds that 'Anger is an appropriate response when one is confronted with the devastating effects of disease.'

6. Ivan Mann (ed.), *The Golden Key*, (Northampton, MNDA, 1990).

7. Phyllis Calvert in *The Golden Key*.

8. Martin Israel, *Dark Victory*, (London, Mowbray, 1995), p. 92.

9. Richard Holloway, *Dancing at the Edge* (London, Fount, 1997), p. 61.

10. Carl Rogers identifies three core conditions for a therapeutic relationship – congruence, empathetic understanding and unconditional positive regard. See Carl Rogers, *On Becoming a Person*, London, Constable, 1997), p. 61f. See also Sheila Cassidy, *The Loneliest Journey*, (London, DLT, 1995), p. 182.

11. Quoted in Bill Kirkpatrick (ed.), *Cry Love, Cry Hope* (London, DLT, 1994), p. 4.

12. Rogers, p. 52.

13. Rogers, p. 61f. See also p. 17: 'I find I am more effective when I can listen acceptingly to myself, and be myself.'

15. Shusaku Endo, *Silence* (London, Quartet 1978), p. 297

16. Martin Israel, p. 60.

17. Sheila Cassidy *The Loneliest Journey*, p. 195.

18. See chapter 2.

19. See e.g. Elisabeth Kubler-Ross, *On Death and Dying* (London, Tavistock 1979), p. 44ff. Colin Murray-Parkes, *Bereavement* (London, Penguin, 1975), pp. 100ff.

20. Alistair V. Campbell, *The Gospel of Anger* (London, SPCK, 1986), p. 95 and 97.

21. See e.g. Sheila Cassidy, p. 198.

22. Elisabeth Kubler-Ross, *The Wheel of Life* (London, Transworld, 1997), p. 120.

23. For another example of the importance of touch see Brian Keenan, *An Evil Cradling*, p. 88.

24. Brian Keenan, *An Evil Cradling*, p. 172.

25. ibid. p. 245.

26. See e.g. Henri Nouwen, *Clowning in Rome* (New York, Doubleday, 1979), p. 2f. Also Martin Israel, *Dark Victory* p. 84, 'I thank God for the ministry of humorists, comedians and clowns. By their outrageous assaults on the apparent normality of everyday life, they cause me to draw breath, and in that action I draw in something of the mystery of God also. When I lose rigid control of my own propriety, I attain an openness . . .'

27. The mystic Meister Eckhart (c.1260–1327) discovered a God who laughs. See Wanda Nash, *Come, Let Us Play!* (London, DLT, 1999) p. 79.

28. Jackie and I made a pact that between 9.30p.m. and 10.30p.m. she would not disturb me. I could have a bath, pray, watch TV and know the space was sacred.

29. ibid. p. 167.

30. Kahlil Gibran, *The Prophet* (London, Arkana, 1992), p. 58.

31. Michael Ignatieff, *Scar Tissue* (London, Vintage, 1994), p. 137.

32. ibid. p. 135.

CHAPTER 8: SHARING THE SUFFERING OF GOD

1. R. S. Thomas, *Collected Poems 1945–1990* (London, J. M. Dent, 1993), p. 104.

2. Richard Wurmbrand, *Sermons in Solitary Confinement* (London, Hodder & Stoughton, 1969), p. 185f.

3. Donald Nicholl, *The Beatitude of Truth* (London, DLT, 1997), p. 64.

4. Simone Weil, *Waiting On God* (Glasgow, Collins, 1951), p. 82–3.

5. See e.g. Brendan Smith, *The Silence of Divine Love* (London, DLT, 1998) to which I am much indebted in this chapter. See also Vanessa Herrick and Ivan Mann, *Jesus Wept* (London, DLT, 1998) Chapter 14 for an exploration of this theme of 'interillumination' in the context of worship. Also 'If the Eye of the Heart were fully open, and we had attained complete Divine Knowledge, we would see that these contraries are all contained finally in an all embracing *unity*; God and man,

pleasure and pain, success and failure are all ultimately one in God. Cyprian Smith, *The Way of Paradox* (London, DLT, 1987), p. 26.

6. Brenda Callaghan, 'What does it mean to belong?' in *The Way* (London, The Way Publications, April 1998), p. 112

7. Etty Hillesum, *An Interrupted Life* (London, Persephone, 1999), quoted in Brendan Smith, p. 73.

8. D. H. Lawrence, *The Complete Poems* (London, Penguin, 1980), p. 727. Reproduced by permission of Laurence Pollinger Ltd. and the estate of Frieda Lawrence Ravagli.

9. Vanessa Herrick and Ivan Mann, *Jesus Wept*, p. 7.

10. I am much indebted to Walter Brueggemann, *Hopeful Imagination* (London, SCM, 1992) for his insights into the ministry of Jeremiah.

11. ibid. p. 14.

12. Martin Israel says that this is the God discovered by those who have suffered much too. See Martin Israel, *Gethsemane* (London, Fount, 1987) p. 25: 'To proceed to traverse the valley of the shadow of death in faith, grasping blindly in the thick darkness, is to know God in a very different way from that proclaimed in traditional religion or conventional piety. This new manifestation of the divine fills the soul with hope . . .'

13. Walter Brueggemann, pp. 22, 23.

14. Michael Ramsey, *The Glory of God and the Transfiguration of Christ* (Longman Green, 1949), p. 146.

15. Paul Ricoeur quoted in Walter Brueggemann, p. 25.

16. ibid. p. 47.

17. From *The Collected Works of St John of the Cross*, trans. Kieran Kavanaugh and Otilio Rodriguez, © 1979, 1991, p. 57f. by Washington Province of Discalced Carmelites, ICS Publications, 2131 Lincoln Road, N.E., Washington, D.C., 20002–1199, U.S.A.

18. Jurgen Moltmann, *The Crucified God* (London, SCM Press, 1974), p. 272.

19. Isaac Watts, from the hymn 'When I survey the wondrous Cross'.

20. Quoted in Walter Brueggemann, p. 25.

21. See Vanessa Herrick and Ivan Mann, *Jesus Wept* (London, DLT, 1998), p. 5: 'For the sake of clarity we shall define vulnerability as: An openness to being wounded (physical or otherwise) which is motivated by love of God and is the outcome of a voluntary relinquishment of the power to protect oneself from being wounded.'

22. Pskov, mid-16th century in *Gates of Mystery: The Art of Holy Russia* (Cambridge, The Lutterworth Press), p. 220.

23. ibid. p. 221

24. Mother Thekla in Ivan Mann (ed.), *The Golden Key*, p. 75.

25. Moltmann, *The Crucified God*, p. 1f.

26. Quoted in Moltmann, p. 48.

27. Cyprian Smith, *The Way of Paradox*, (London, DLT, 1987), p. 27.

28. Sara Maitland, *Virgin Territory* (London, Pavane, 1985), p. 68f.

CHAPTER 9: SUFFERING, LIFE AND PRAYER

1. Robert van de Weyer and Pat Saunders, *The Easter Spirit*, (London, DLT, 1990), p. 70.

2. From Swinburne, 'Hertha'.

3. Throughout, I use this word rather than 'church' or 'fellowship', to be clear what Christian community is essentially about and to free us from associations brought to mind by the more familiar words.

4. See pp. 105ff.

5. Johannes B. Metz, *Poverty of Spirit* (New York, Paulist Press), p. 23f.

6. Quoted in John Moses, *The Desert* (Noraice, The Canterbury Press, 1997), p. 63.

7. The following section is a meditation that has been growing over many years. It owes its origin to a study of Simon Tugwell[1] *Reflections on the Beatitudes* (London, DLT, 1980) but there are many other lesser influences to which I owe a large debt.

8. See also chapter 7 note 4 and R. S. Thomas, *Collected Poems 1945–1990* (London, J. M. Dent, 1993), p. 220

9. Joachim Jeremias, *The Sermon on the Mount* (London, Athlone Press, 1961), p. 32f, summarises the Sermon on the Mount by saying, 'You are forgiven; you are the child of God; you belong to His kingdom. The sun of righteousness has risen over your life. You no longer belong to yourself; rather, you belong to the city of God, the light of which shines in the darkness. Now you may experience it: out of the thankfulness of a redeemed child of God a new life is growing.'

10. See chapter 7.

11. See p. 78.

12. Karl Barth, *Church Dogmatics IV.1.* (Edinburgh, T & T Clark, 1956), p. 185.

13. Brendan Smith, *The Silence of Divine Love* (London, DLT, 1998), p. 68.

14. In secular Greek the word meant partnership, alliance, association.

15. Mother Mary Clare, *Encountering the Depths* (London, DLT, 1981), p. 55. See also the quote from Mother Mary Clare in chapter 3, p. 41.

16. See chapter 2.

17. Francis de Sales used the terms 'the signified will of God' and the 'will of God's good pleasure'. The second of these may give the impression that the situation we are in is Godswill. In fact the opposite may be the case so I have avoided this term in favour of 'the inherent will of God'. See Francis de Sales, Jane de Chantal, *Letters of Spiritual Direction* (New York, Paulist Press, 1988), p. 41f.

18. *Koinonia* has to be involved in discerning the will of God. True vocation is discovered when the inner promptings of the heart find reflection in what the *koinonia* discerns in us – or vice versa.

19. Francis de Sales, Jane de Chantal p. 42.

20. ibid. p. 42.
    Sheila Cassidy, *Sharing the Darkness* (London, DLT, 1988), p. 92–4. My own experience of looking after a wife who had motor neurone disease was similar. She came to accept the limitations of the disease – a struggling rather than a passive acceptance. She wrote, 'My spirit has always been much larger than my body, somehow the largest part of me. Much bigger than this body which now lies resting, resting. I cannot walk far or climb stairs let alone mountains – but this spirit knows no bounds. . . . Imprisoned within this frail body I am still as free as a bird, with a song to sing'. Ivan Mann (ed.), *The Golden Key*, p. 79. See also Virginia Thesiger, 'The Healing', quoted in chapter 2.

CHAPTER 10: REACHING BEYOND SUFFERING

1. W.H.Auden, *Collected Poems* (London, Faber & Faber, 1976), p. 141.

2. H.A. Williams, *Some Day I'll Find You,* (London, Fount, 1984), p. 177.

3. This subject is not explored further in this book, simply because there are no words. Those who offer their suffering to God in this way hardly speak about it. I actually think that little *can* be said.

4. a term used by the Orthodox theologian Paul Edvokimov, *L'Orthodoxie* (Neutchatel, Delachaux et Nestle, 1959), p. 113.

5. A term used by St Benedict which implies both a change of way of living – inner attitude and outward behaviour, but also a transformation of the person. See Cyprian Smith, *The Path of Life* (York, Ampleforth Abbey Press, 1995), p. 27.

6. See the distinction between signing on and signing off in chapter 9 and the discussion of active/passive in chapter 2.

7. Iain Matthew, *The Impact of God* (London, Hodder & Stoughton, 1995), p. 93, reproduced by permission of Hodder & Stoughton. I am very much indebted to Iain Matthew and his writing especially in this chapter.

8. ibid. p. 113.

9. *St John of the Cross*, pp. 404–6.

10. Iain Matthew, p. 57.

11. Iain Matthew, p. 85.

12. St John of the Cross p. 67.
13. Artur Weiser, *The Psalms* (London, SCM, 192), p. 359. Commenting on Psalm 44 Artur Weiser writes, 'But because the reason for man's suffering and its purpose are hidden in God . . . he is for that very reason the only one who in that situation is able to help man to endure.'
14. Moltmann, *The Crucified God*, p. 4.
15. St John of the Cross, p. 172.
16. William Johnston, *Being In Love* (London, Fount, 1988), p. 89.
17. St John of the Cross, p. 143.
18. ibid. p. 96.
19. Maria Boulding, *The Coming of God* (London, Fount, 1984), p. 8, quoted more fully in chapter 11, p. 154.
20. Iain Matthew, p. 76.
21. St John of the Cross, p. 482. 'You do very well, O soul, to seek him ever as one hidden. . . However surely it may seem that you find, experience, and understand God, because he is inaccessible and concealed you must always regard him as hidden, and serve him who is hidden in a secret way. Do not be like the many foolish ones who, in their lowly understanding of God, think that when they do not understand, taste, or experience him, he is far away and utterly concealed. The contrary belief would be truer . . . You do well, then, at all times in both adversity and prosperity, to consider God as hidden . . . and call after him thus: Where have you hidden Beloved, and left me moaning.'
22. Cyprian Smith, *The Way of Paradox*.
23. Moltmann, *The Crucified God*, p. 19.
24. Iain Matthew, p. 10.
25. The question of timing is explored more in chapter 11.
26. St John of the Cross, p. 421.
27. Anthony de Mello, *Sadhana* (Anand, Gujarat Sahitya Prakash, 1978), p. 27.
28. St John of the Cross, p. 63f.
29. See Louis J. Puhl S. J., *The Spiritual Exercises of St Ignatius* (Chicago, Loyola University Press, 1951), p. 35, [75].
30. Philip Sheldrake (ed.), *The Way of Ignatius Loyola*, (London, SPCK, 1991), p. 48.
31. Karl Rahner, source unknown.
32. This poem represents my 'Toledo' experience. Driven to exhaustion and beyond myself with aching grief I sat down to pray, saw a crucifix and realised that I loved God from somewhere too deep for words, beyond any human reasoning. I wrote the poem in a few minutes and have pondered its significance ever since.

CHAPTER 11: SUFFERING AND SILENCE

1. Source unknown.
2. Simon Bailey, *The Well Within* (London, DLT, 1996).
3. Exact reference unknown. See Bonhoeffer, *Letters and Papers from Prison* p. 176.
4. St John of the Cross, p. 425.
5. Archie Hill, *Closed World Of Love* (London, Futura, 1976), p. 101.
6. ibid, p. 109.
7. See Kathleen Fischer, *Transforming Fire* (New York, Paulist Press, 1999), p. 139 and Sheila Cassidy, *Sharing The Darkness*, p. 65.
8. R. S. Thomas, *Collected Poems 1945–1990* (London, J. M. Dent, 1993),p. 361.
9. 'Via Negativa', ibid. p. 220.
10. Denise Levertov, *Sands Of The Well* (New York, New Directions, 1996), quoted in Fischer p. 89. © Denise Levertov, reprinted by permission of New Directions Publishing Corporation.
11. Martin Israel, *Living Alone* (London, SPCK, 1982), p. 15
12. Martin Israel, *Dark Victory* (London, Mowbray, 1995), p. 3.
13. ibid. p. 8.
14. See chapter 12 for a similar picture of a battlefield of words.

15. This phrase was originally coined by William Styron. Borrowed from Jim Cotter, *Brainsquall* (Sheffield, Cairns Publications, 1997) p. xxi.
16. As I reflect I realise the phrase 'somnambulant rage' comes from Brian Keenan, *An Evil Cradling*, p. 68. For me it reflects the sense of being 'dead', aware of immense pain, feeling it and yet not feeling it.
17. By 'you' is meant anyone who will just be alongside – a companion in waiting.
18. *Vulgate Version 1 Kings 19.*
19. 'Keep thy mind in hell and despair not', Staretz Silouan in Archimandrite Sophrony *The Monk of Mount Athos*, p. 116.
20. A day in London took me past Lambeth Palace and the Church Commissioners buildings. I thought I was coming out of a depression. In fact I went much deeper and produced this poem.
21. R. S. Thomas, *No Truce With The Furies* (Newcastle upon Tyne, Bloodaxe, 1995), p. 19.
22. Source unknown.
23. T. S. Eliot, *Little Gidding IV, The Complete Poems and Plays of T. S. Eliot* (London, Faber & Faber, 1969),p. 196.
24. W.B.Yeats, The Second Coming, *The Poems* (London, J.M.Dent, 1990),p. 235.
25. Iain Matthew, *The Impact of God*, p. 36f.
26. Source unknown.
27. See Jurgen Moltmann, *The Experiment Hope* (London, SCM, 1975), p. 51.
28. Dag Hammarskjold, *Markings* (London, Faber & Faber, 1964), p. 31.
29. Charles Peguy quoted in Moltmann, p. 189.
30. Etty Hillesum, *An Interrupted Life and Letters from Westerbork* (New York, Henry Holt, 1996), pp. 287f, 294.
31. James L. Empereur, *Spirituality and the Gay Person*, p. 49.
32. Precepts Chapter 1, quoted in Angela Partington (ed.), *The Oxford Dictionary of Quotations* (Oxford, OUP, 1996), p. 339.
33. Mary Craig, *Blessings* (London, Coronet, 1979), p. 36.
34. ibid. p. 47, 49.
35. ibid. p. 50.
36. Maria Boulding, *The Coming of God*, p. 7f.

CHAPTER 12: SUFFERING AND CREATIVITY
1. Christopher Nolan, *Dam-Burst of Dreams* (London, Weidenfeld & Nicolson, 1982), p. 146. '*The Sunday Times* launched an appeal for funds to purchase a computer for me. . . . the Christopher Nolan Trust was set up, and all surplus funds from the appeal were at my request allocated to the providing of computerised equipment for other tongue-tied disabled people.'
2. See chapter 2.
3. James L. Empereur, *Spiritual Direction and the Gay Person*, chapters 7, 8, 9.
4. ibid. p. 153.
5. Rowan Williams, *Open to Judgement*, p. 91, 'As Augustine might have said, the only integration we can achieve in this life is the knowledge that we cannot achieve integration, and the fullest maturity is to know our immaturity'.
6. Dag Hammarskjold, *Markings*, p. 62.
7. Moltmann, *The Crucified God*, p. 1.
8. Brian Keenan, *An Evil Cradling*, pp. 222–234.
9. Kathleen Fischer, *Transforming Fire*, p. 167. Quoting Barbara Denning, Fischer suggests that part of the way of non-violence is to say to the oppressor, 'You are not the other, and I am not the other. I will not cast you out of the human race.'
10. Desmond Tutu, *No Future Without Forgiveness*, p. 20.
11. In Peter King, *Dark Night Spirituality* (London, SPCK, 1995), p. 66.
12. Richard Stilgoe in Ivan Mann, *Never 'eard of it* (Northampton, MNDA, 1991) p. 59.
13. It was the best piece of advice I had as I wrote this book.
14. Peter King, pp. 57–9.

15. Peter King, p. 37.
16. Brian Keenan, *An Evil Cradling*, p. 68f.
17. 'I and My Rose', G. A. Studdert Kennedy, *The Unutterable Beauty* (London, Hodder & Stoughton, 1964), p. 97.
18. *Poems of Gerard Manley Hopkins*, p. 95.
19. Ann Griffiths, 'I Saw Him Standing', in Rowan Williams, *After Silent Centuries* (Oxford, Perpetua Press, 1994) p. 46.
20. Jane Grayshon, *Treasures in Darkness* (London, Hodder & Stoughton, 1996), p. 65.
21. Enid Hencke in Cicely Saunders, *Beyond All Pain* (London, SPCK, 1983) p. 10.
22. See, e.g. Carl Rogers and Gerry Hughes.
23. Etty Hillesum, *An Interrupted Life and Letters from Westerbork*, pp. 250.
24. I am grateful to Rachel Verney for letting me watch this excerpt of her work.
25. 'The Annunciation' in Edwin Muir, *Collected Poems*, (London, Faber & Faber, 1979), p. 117.
26. Christy Brown, *My Left Foot* (London, Mandarin, 1954), p. 56f., 80
27. Gary Ansdell, *Music For Life* (London, Kingsley, 1995), p. 15.
28. ibid.p. 18.
29. ibid.p. 17.
30. ibid.p. 17.
31. ibid. p. 35.
32. ibid. p. 18.
33. Iain Matthew, *The Impact of God* (London, Hodder & Stoughton, 1995), p. 78.
34. ibid. p. 106.
35. Gary Ansdell, p. 134.
36. Etty Hillesum, *An Interrupted Life and Letters from Westerbork*, p. 332
37. *Rule for a New Brother*, (London, DLT, 1973), p. 54f.
38. Michael Ignatieff, *Scar Tissue*, pp. 136ff.

INDEX